Online Resources

Included with your purchase are multiple online resources. This includes the practice tests in an interactive format and a convenient study timer to help you manage your time.

Instructions for accessing these resources can be found on the last page of this book.

Ham Radio License Manual for the General Exam

425+ Practice Questions and Ham Radio Book [For the 2022-2026 Question Set]

Lydia Morrison

Copyright © 2024 by TPB Publishing

All rights reserved. No part of this publication may be reproduced, distributed, or transmitted in any form or by any means, including photocopying, recording, or other electronic or mechanical methods, without the prior written permission of the publisher, except in the case of brief quotations embodied in critical reviews and certain other noncommercial uses permitted by copyright law.

Written and edited by TPB Publishing.

TPB Publishing is not associated with or endorsed by any official testing organization. TPB Publishing is a publisher of unofficial educational products. All test and organization names are trademarks of their respective owners. Content in this book is included for utilitarian purposes only and does not constitute an endorsement by TPB Publishing of any particular point of view.

ISBN 13: 9781637754900

Table of Contents

Welcome 1

Quick Overview 2

Test-Taking Strategies 3

Introduction 7

Study Prep Plan for the HAM Radio Test................................. 8

Subelement G1 – Commission's Rules 11

Subelement G2 – Operating Procedures 36

Subelement G3 – Radio Wave Propagation 60

Subelement G3 – Questions 70

Subelement G4 – Amateur Radio Practices.......................... 77

Subelement G5 – Electrical Principles 93

Subelement G6 – Circuit Components 109

Subelement G7 – Practical Circuits 121

Subelement G8 – Signals and Emissions............................ 134

Subelement G9 – Antennas and Feed Lines 148

Subelement G0 – Electrical and RF Safety 160

Index 168

Online Resources.. 174

Welcome

Dear Reader,

Welcome to your new Test Prep Books study guide! We are pleased that you chose us to help you prepare for your exam. There are many study options to choose from, and we appreciate you choosing us. Studying can be a daunting task, but we have designed a smart, effective study guide to help prepare you for what lies ahead.

Whether you're a parent helping your child learn and grow, a high school student working hard to get into your dream college, or a nursing student studying for a complex exam, we want to help give you the tools you need to succeed. We hope this study guide gives you the skills and the confidence to thrive, and we can't thank you enough for allowing us to be part of your journey.

In an effort to continue to improve our products, we welcome feedback from our customers. We look forward to hearing from you. Suggestions, success stories, and criticisms can all be communicated by emailing us at support@testprepbooks.com.

Sincerely,

Test Prep Books Team

Quick Overview

As you draw closer to taking your exam, effective preparation becomes more and more important. Thankfully, you have this study guide to help you get ready. Use this guide to help keep your studying on track and refer to it often.

This study guide contains several key sections that will help you be successful on your exam. The guide contains tips for what you should do the night before and the day of the test. Also included are test-taking tips. Knowing the right information is not always enough. Many well-prepared test takers struggle with exams. These tips will help equip you to accurately read, assess, and answer test questions.

A large part of the guide is devoted to showing you what content to expect on the exam and to helping you better understand that content. In this guide are practice test questions so that you can see how well you have grasped the content. Then, answer explanations are provided so that you can understand why you missed certain questions.

Don't try to cram the night before you take your exam. This is not a wise strategy for a few reasons. First, your retention of the information will be low. Your time would be better used by reviewing information you already know rather than trying to learn a lot of new information. Second, you will likely become stressed as you try to gain a large amount of knowledge in a short amount of time. Third, you will be depriving yourself of sleep. So be sure to go to bed at a reasonable time the night before. Being well-rested helps you focus and remain calm.

Be sure to eat a substantial breakfast the morning of the exam. If you are taking the exam in the afternoon, be sure to have a good lunch as well. Being hungry is distracting and can make it difficult to focus. You have hopefully spent lots of time preparing for the exam. Don't let an empty stomach get in the way of success!

When travelling to the testing center, leave earlier than needed. That way, you have a buffer in case you experience any delays. This will help you remain calm and will keep you from missing your appointment time at the testing center.

Be sure to pace yourself during the exam. Don't try to rush through the exam. There is no need to risk performing poorly on the exam just so you can leave the testing center early. Allow yourself to use all of the allotted time if needed.

Remain positive while taking the exam even if you feel like you are performing poorly. Thinking about the content you should have mastered will not help you perform better on the exam.

Once the exam is complete, take some time to relax. Even if you feel that you need to take the exam again, you will be well served by some down time before you begin studying again. It's often easier to convince yourself to study if you know that it will come with a reward!

Test-Taking Strategies

1. Predicting the Answer

When you feel confident in your preparation for a multiple-choice test, try predicting the answer before reading the answer choices. This is especially useful on questions that test objective factual knowledge. By predicting the answer before reading the available choices, you eliminate the possibility that you will be distracted or led astray by an incorrect answer choice. You will feel more confident in your selection if you read the question, predict the answer, and then find your prediction among the answer choices. After using this strategy, be sure to still read all of the answer choices carefully and completely. If you feel unprepared, you should not attempt to predict the answers. This would be a waste of time and an opportunity for your mind to wander in the wrong direction.

2. Reading the Whole Question

Too often, test takers scan a multiple-choice question, recognize a few familiar words, and immediately jump to the answer choices. Test authors are aware of this common impatience, and they will sometimes prey upon it. For instance, a test author might subtly turn the question into a negative, or he or she might redirect the focus of the question right at the end. The only way to avoid falling into these traps is to read the entirety of the question carefully before reading the answer choices.

3. Looking for Wrong Answers

Long and complicated multiple-choice questions can be intimidating. One way to simplify a difficult multiple-choice question is to eliminate all of the answer choices that are clearly wrong. In most sets of answers, there will be at least one selection that can be dismissed right away. If the test is administered on paper, the test taker could draw a line through it to indicate that it may be ignored; otherwise, the test taker will have to perform this operation mentally or on scratch paper. In either case, once the obviously incorrect answers have been eliminated, the remaining choices may be considered. Sometimes identifying the clearly wrong answers will give the test taker some information about the correct answer. For instance, if one of the remaining answer choices is a direct opposite of one of the eliminated answer choices, it may well be the correct answer. The opposite of obviously wrong is obviously right! Of course, this is not always the case. Some answers are obviously incorrect simply because they are irrelevant to the question being asked. Still, identifying and eliminating some incorrect answer choices is a good way to simplify a multiple-choice question.

4. Don't Overanalyze

Anxious test takers often overanalyze questions. When you are nervous, your brain will often run wild, causing you to make associations and discover clues that don't actually exist. If you feel that this may be a problem for you, do whatever you can to slow down during the test. Try taking a deep breath or counting to ten. As you read and consider the question, restrict yourself to the particular words used by the author. Avoid thought tangents about what the author *really* meant, or what he or she was *trying* to say. The only things that matter on a multiple-choice test are the words that are actually in the question. You must avoid reading too much into a multiple-choice question, or supposing that the writer meant something other than what he or she wrote.

5. No Need for Panic

It is wise to learn as many strategies as possible before taking a multiple-choice test, but it is likely that you will come across a few questions for which you simply don't know the answer. In this situation, avoid panicking. Because most multiple-choice tests include dozens of questions, the relative value of a single wrong answer is small. As much as possible, you should compartmentalize each question on a multiple-choice test. In other words, you should not allow your feelings about one question to affect your success on the others. When you find a question that you either don't understand or don't know how to answer, just take a deep breath and do your best. Read the entire question slowly and carefully. Try rephrasing the question a couple of different ways. Then, read all of the answer choices carefully. After eliminating obviously wrong answers, make a selection and move on to the next question.

6. Confusing Answer Choices

When working on a difficult multiple-choice question, there may be a tendency to focus on the answer choices that are the easiest to understand. Many people, whether consciously or not, gravitate to the answer choices that require the least concentration, knowledge, and memory. This is a mistake. When you come across an answer choice that is confusing, you should give it extra attention. A question might be confusing because you do not know the subject matter to which it refers. If this is the case, don't

eliminate the answer before you have affirmatively settled on another. When you come across an answer choice of this type, set it aside as you look at the remaining choices. If you can confidently assert that one of the other choices is correct, you can leave the confusing answer aside. Otherwise, you will need to take a moment to try to better understand the confusing answer choice. Rephrasing is one way to tease out the sense of a confusing answer choice.

7. Your First Instinct

Many people struggle with multiple-choice tests because they overthink the questions. If you have studied sufficiently for the test, you should be prepared to trust your first instinct once you have carefully and completely read the question and all of the answer choices. There is a great deal of research suggesting that the mind can come to the correct conclusion very quickly once it has obtained all of the relevant information. At times, it may seem to you as if your intuition is working faster even than your reasoning mind. This may in fact be true. The knowledge you obtain while studying may be retrieved from your subconscious before you have a chance to work out the associations that support it. Verify your instinct by working out the reasons that it should be trusted.

8. Key Words

Many test takers struggle with multiple-choice questions because they have poor reading comprehension skills. Quickly reading and understanding a multiple-choice question requires a mixture of skill and experience. To help with this, try jotting down a few key words and phrases on a piece of scrap paper. Doing this concentrates the process of reading and forces the mind to weigh the relative importance of the question's parts. In selecting words and phrases to write down, the test taker thinks about the question more deeply and carefully. This is especially true for multiple-choice questions that are preceded by a long prompt.

9. Subtle Negatives

One of the oldest tricks in the multiple-choice test writer's book is to subtly reverse the meaning of a question with a word like *not* or *except*. If you are not paying attention to each word in the question, you can easily be led astray by this trick. For instance, a common question format is, "Which of the following is...?" Obviously, if the question instead is, "Which of the following is not...?," then the answer will be quite different. Even worse, the test makers are aware of the potential for this mistake and will include one answer choice that would be correct if the question were not negated or reversed. A test taker who misses the reversal will find what he or she believes to be a correct answer and will be so confident that he or she will fail to reread the question and discover the original error. The only way to avoid this is to practice a wide variety of multiple-choice questions and to pay close attention to each and every word.

10. Reading Every Answer Choice

It may seem obvious, but you should always read every one of the answer choices! Too many test takers fall into the habit of scanning the question and assuming that they understand the question because they recognize a few key words. From there, they pick the first answer choice that answers the question they believe they have read. Test takers who read all of the answer choices might discover that one of the latter answer choices is actually *more* correct. Moreover, reading all of the answer choices can remind you of facts related to the question that can help you arrive at the correct answer. Sometimes, a misstatement or incorrect detail in one of the latter answer choices will trigger your memory of the subject and will enable you to find the right answer. Failing to read all of the answer choices is like not reading all of the items on a restaurant menu: you might miss out on the perfect choice.

11. Spot the Hedges

One of the keys to success on multiple-choice tests is paying close attention to every word. This is never truer than with words like *almost*, *most*, *some*, and *sometimes*. These words are called "hedges" because they indicate that a statement is not totally true or not true in every place and time. An absolute statement will contain no hedges, but in many subjects, the answers are not always straightforward or absolute. There are always exceptions to the rules in these subjects. For this reason,

you should favor those multiple-choice questions that contain hedging language. The presence of qualifying words indicates that the author is taking special care with his or her words, which is certainly important when composing the right answer. After all, there are many ways to be wrong, but there is only one way to be right! For this reason, it is wise to avoid answers that are absolute when taking a multiple-choice test. An absolute answer is one that says things are either all one way or all another. They often include words like *every*, *always*, *best*, and *never*. If you are taking a multiple-choice test in a subject that doesn't lend itself to absolute answers, be on your guard if you see any of these words.

12. Long Answers

In many subject areas, the answers are not simple. As already mentioned, the right answer often requires hedges. Another common feature of the answers to a complex or subjective question are qualifying clauses, which are groups of words that subtly modify the meaning of the sentence. If the question or answer choice describes a rule to which there are exceptions or the subject matter is complicated, ambiguous, or confusing, the correct answer will require many words in order to be expressed clearly and accurately. In essence, you should not be deterred by answer choices that seem excessively long. Oftentimes, the author of the text will not be able to write the correct answer without offering some qualifications and modifications. Your job is to read the answer choices thoroughly and completely and to select the one that most accurately and precisely answers the question.

13. Restating to Understand

Sometimes, a question on a multiple-choice test is difficult not because of what it asks but because of how it is written. If this is the case, restate the question or answer choice in different words. This process serves a couple of important purposes. First, it forces you to concentrate on the core of the question. In order to rephrase the question accurately, you have to understand it well. Rephrasing the question will concentrate your mind on the key words and ideas. Second, it will present the information to your mind in a fresh way. This process may trigger your memory and render some useful scrap of information picked up while studying.

14. True Statements

Sometimes an answer choice will be true in itself, but it does not answer the question. This is one of the main reasons why it is essential to read the question carefully and completely before proceeding to the answer choices. Too often, test takers skip ahead to the answer choices and look for true statements. Having found one of these, they are content to select it without reference to the question above. The savvy test taker will always read the entire question before turning to the answer choices. Then, having settled on a correct answer choice, he or she will refer to the original question and ensure that the selected answer is relevant. The mistake of choosing a correct-but-irrelevant answer choice is especially common on questions related to specific pieces of objective knowledge.

15. No Patterns

One of the more dangerous ideas that circulates about multiple-choice tests is that the correct answers tend to fall into patterns. These erroneous ideas range from a belief that B and C are the most common right answers, to the idea that an unprepared test-taker should answer "A-B-A-C-A-D-A-B-A." It cannot be emphasized enough that pattern-seeking of this type is exactly the WRONG way to approach a multiple-choice test. To begin with, it is highly unlikely that the test maker will plot the correct answers according to some predetermined pattern. The questions are scrambled and delivered in a random order. Furthermore, even if the test maker was following a pattern in the assignation of correct answers, there is no reason why the test taker would know which pattern he or she was using. Any attempt to discern a pattern in the answer choices is a waste of time and a distraction from the real work of taking the test. A test taker would be much better served by extra preparation before the test than by reliance on a pattern in the answers.

Introduction

Function of the Test

The HAM Radio General Test is one of three licensing exams the FCC offers for amateur radio operators. It represents intermediate proficiency in amateur radio. To earn a general license, candidates must first pass the Technician licensing exam. Once they pass the test, earning their general radio credentials, candidates become eligible for the most advanced amateur radio credential the FCC offers, the Amateur Extra license. General license holders maintain all privileges available to Technician licensees. Additionally, they receive access to more high frequency, or shortwave, radio bands; these expanded allocation privileges allow General class operators to communicate with users in other countries. General class operators have access to all radio bands allocated to hams and can communicate in any operating mode. However, they have some privilege limitations when communicating on allocated amateur bands.

Test Administration

Anyone is eligible to earn a US amateur radio license, except government representatives from other countries. License-holding volunteer examiners (VEs) administer accredited amateur radio licensing tests on behalf of the FCC across the country. Exam registration costs $15.00, and test-takers can take all three licensing exams on the same day in order. In other words, they can take the Technician exam, and if they pass, they then earn the opportunity to take the General exam. Subsequently, they become eligible to take the Amateur Extra licensing test. The FCC requires the presence of three license-holding examiners to administer an exam. Each VE must have a valid license in the class above that of the given exam. Candidates can choose between online or in-person testing. Once earned, US licenses remain valid for 10 years then become eligible for renewal.

Test Format

Each FCC amateur radio licensing exam has a question pool generated collectively by VEs. The question pools for each licensing class are updated every four years. The HAM Radio General Exam has 35 multiple-choice questions out of 452 potential questions in the pool. Each query has four possible answer choices. To ensure the test covers every topic, one question is chosen from each subject represented in the question pool to comprise the test content. The question pool was most recently revised on July 1, 2023.

Scoring

To pass the exam, the test-taker must get at least 26 questions correct, which means the candidate must answer 74% of the questions correctly to receive their license. Candidates that pass are given a Certificate of Successful Completion of Examination (CSCE), which expires after 365 days. The VEs submit the test results to the FCC, and successful test-takers receive their updated credentials in the online database within one week. However, they may operate with their newly earned privileges immediately using a temporary adaptation of their callsign to show they await official General licensing.

Study Prep Plan for the HAM Radio Test

1 **Schedule** - Use one of our study schedules below or come up with one of your own.

2 **Relax** - Test anxiety can hurt even the best students. There are many ways to reduce stress. Find the one that works best for you.

3 **Execute** - Once you have a good plan in place, be sure to stick to it.

One Week Study Schedule

Day 1	Subelement G1 - Commission's Rules
Day 2	Subelement G2 - Operating Procedures
Day 3	Subelement G3 - Radio Wave Propagation
Day 4	Subelement G4 - Amateur Radio Practices
Day 5	Subelement G6 - Circuit Components
Day 6	Subelement G8 - Signals and Emissions
Day 7	Take Your Exam!

Two Week Study Schedule

Day 1	Subelement G1 - Commission's Rules	Day 8	Subelement G5 - Electrical Principles
Day 2	G1E	Day 9	Subelement G6 - Circuit Components
Day 3	Subelement G2 - Operating Procedures	Day 10	Subelement G7 - Practical Circuits
Day 4	Subelement G2 - Questions	Day 11	Subelement G8 - Signals and Emissions
Day 5	Subelement G3 - Radio Wave Propagation	Day 12	Subelement G9 - Antennas and Feed Lines
Day 6	G3C	Day 13	Subelement G0 - Electrical and RF Safety
Day 7	Subelement G4 - Amateur Radio Practices	Day 14	Take Your Exam!

Study Prep Plan for the HAM Radio Test

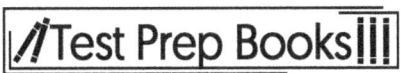

One Month Study Schedule	Day 1	Subelement G1 - Commission's Rules	Day 11	Subelement G3 - Questions	Day 21	Subelement G7 - Practical Circuits
	Day 2	G1C	Day 12	Subelement G4 - Amateur Radio...	Day 22	Digital Sign Processing (DSP)
	Day 3	G1D	Day 13	Subelement G4 - Questions	Day 23	Subelement G8 - Signals and Emissions
	Day 4	Subelement G1 - Questions	Day 14	Subelement G5 - Electrical Principles	Day 24	G8B
	Day 5	Subelement G2 - Operating Procedures	Day 15	G5B	Day 25	Subelement G8 - Questions
	Day 6	G2C	Day 16	G5C	Day 26	Subelement G9 - Antennas and Feed Lines
	Day 7	G2D	Day 17	Subelement G5 - Questions	Day 27	Subelement G9 - Questions
	Day 8	Subelement G2 - Questions	Day 18	Subelement G6 - Circuit Components	Day 28	Subelement G0 - Electrical and RF Safety
	Day 9	Subelement G3 - Radio Wave Propagation	Day 19	G6B	Day 29	Subelement G0 - Questions
	Day 10	G3B	Day 20	Subelement G6 - Questions	Day 30	Take Your Exam!

Build your own prep plan by visiting the Online Resources page.

Instructions and a QR code can be found on the last page of this guide.

Subelement G1 – Commission's Rules

G1A

General Class Control Operator Frequency Privileges

Electromagnetic radiation occurs when electric and magnetic fields oscillate perpendicular to each other in synchronicity, generating **electromagnetic waves**. Changes in either the electric or magnetic field influence the power produced as electrically charged particles accelerate; consequently, these shifts affect the character of the waveforms in the electromagnetic field. The **electromagnetic spectrum** is the range of frequencies for electromagnetic waves. It contains the **radio spectrum**, which includes all **radio frequency (RF)** signals. On the electromagnetic spectrum, radio frequencies occur between audio frequencies, which exist on the low end, and infrared frequencies, which occur on the high end.

Radio waves are a type of sinusoidal waveform that can travel and carry information through many mediums, including vacuums, air, liquids, and solids. They transmit data when a source and a receiver are tuned to the same frequency. Radio waves behave differently when they hit objects depending on the object's properties. **Reflection** happens when the object is bigger than the RF wavelength, which causes the wave to bounce off the object's surface. **Refraction** happens when the object has a higher density than the prior medium and changes the direction the wave is traveling by bouncing the signal at an angle. **Scattering** happens when the object has an odd shape and causes the radio wave to disperse and move in several different directions. **Absorption** happens when the object does not have properties that lead to reflection, refraction, or scattering; therefore, the signal is absorbed and disappears. Radio waves can also be diffracted. **Diffraction** occurs when an object blocks a wave, so the wave separates to travel around the object. These behavioral principles guide **propagation**, or the way radio waves travel.

Radio waves behave like an alternating current. An **alternating current (AC)** is a type of electric current with a waveform characterized by repetitive and continuous directional reversal over time. In other words, the direction of the electric current's movement alternates. An alternating current can be juxtaposed with **direct current (DC),** which continuously moves in a single direction. **Transmitters** generate radio waves, and **transmission lines**, like coaxial cables, carry radio frequency currents.

Frequency refers to the speed of electromagnetic wave oscillations, meaning how many times the alternating current switches direction per second. Put another way, frequency is the number of peaks that occur over a certain temporal distance. Frequency is measured in **Hertz**, or the number of cycles per second. Higher frequencies carry more energy.

Wavelength is how far a radio wave travels during one alternating current cycle. It measures the distance between corresponding points on spatial wave patterns, or the amount of space between each repetitive crest in a periodic wave form. **Amplitude** refers to a waveform's height during the crest phase. A continuous waveform (CW) references a wave that has sustained amplitude and frequency.

There is an inversely proportional relationship between frequencies and wavelengths – higher frequencies mean shorter wavelengths and lower frequencies mean longer wavelengths. To convert a frequency to a wavelength, divide the wavelength (measured in meters [m] = 300) by the frequency (measured in Megahertz [MHz]). The formula looks like:

$$\text{Speed/Frequency} = \text{Wavelength}$$

For example, for a frequency of 10MHz:

$$300m / 10Mhz = 30m$$

A **frequency band** is a particular segment of radio frequencies on the RF spectrum allocated for particular use by the **International Telecommunication Union (ITU)**. Bands are usually categorized by wavelength. Radio frequency bands are broken down as follows:

- VLF – very low frequency (3kHz – 30 kHz)
- LF – low frequency (30 kHz – 300 kHz)
- MF – medium frequency (300 kHz – 3 MHz)
- HF – high frequency (3 MHz – 30 MHz)
- VHF – very high frequency (30 MHz – 300 MHz)
- UHF – ultrahigh frequency (300 MHz – 3 GHz)
- SHF – super high frequency (3 GHz – 30 GHz)
- EHF – extremely high frequency (30 GHz – 300 GHz)

The **Federal Communications Commission (FCC)** is the independent U.S. government agency responsible for regulating radio communications. The FCC determines licensing requirements for amateur radio transmission and sets band and frequency privileges for each license class. **Band privileges** determine who has permission to transmit and receive within certain frequency bands. **Frequency privileges** are the frequencies a license-holding individual may use for transmission based on their license class and communication purpose.

The General class license grants users access to all bands, including high frequency (HF) bands, also known as **shortwave bands**. However, those with a General license do not have access to all frequencies available on every band, since there are certain frequencies reserved for those with an Amateur Extra license. There are also limitations related to the types of transmissions allowed on different bands and frequencies. **Operational modes** refer to the kind of communication being transmitted. One of the most common modes, called a **phone operation**, involves sending a voice signal out. Users can also send images or information resembling images, such as **amateur television (ATV)**, **slow scan television (SSTV)**, and **weather facsimile (WEFAX)**.

There are several key limitations for General class license holders. First, they have frequency privileges for all bands, including the 160m, 60m, 30m, 17m, 12m, and 10m bands. However, on the 30m band (10.1 MHz), phone operation and image transmission are not permitted, and on the 60m band, communication is only allowed on certain channels.

On the 10m band, available frequencies include 28.020 MHz, 28.350 MHz, and 28.550 MHz. **Repeaters** are used on the 10m band to retransmit weaker signals, so they reach frequencies on the upper end, above 29.5 MHz.

On limited bands, the following frequencies are available to General class license holders: 80m (3,560 kHz), 75m (3900 kHz), 40m (7.250 MHz), 20m (14305 kHz), and 15m (21300 kHz). As a rule of thumb,

Subelement G1 – Commission's Rules

General class license holders are allowed in upper frequencies of limited bands for both CW and voice transmissions.

Primary and Secondary Allocations

There are several frequency bands exclusively reserved for amateur radio users. Sometimes, however, amateur frequencies are shared with other types of users. In such cases, the FCC prioritizes the group with more urgent communication needs. **Primary allocations** refer to groups, called primary services, that receive precedence on amateur radio bands. **Secondary allocations** are given to **secondary services**, or groups that have lower priority access. Secondary services are allowed to use shared frequency allocations with the stipulation that they must avoid causing harmful interference for primary services. Additionally, on shared amateur radio bands, secondary users must accept interference from and defer to primary users, meaning if a primary service interferes, the ham user must move to another frequency or halt transmission. All HF and UHF bands include some shared frequency allocations. For example, 30m and 60m bands both have shared frequency arrangements. It's important for hams in the United States to remember that amateur allocations are secondary services in cases of international interference. The FCC publishes the **Table of Frequency Allocations**, which details all frequency allocation information, including allowances for primary and secondary services.

G1B

Antenna structure limitations

Radio antennas are devices that change voltages of a certain frequency into radiating electromagnetic waveforms during transmission and convert radio signals into voltages upon reception. The most common antenna structure is the **dipole**. A dipole has two symmetrical linear poles of equal length protruding in opposite directions from a **central feed line**, usually a coaxial cable. Dipole construction requires a combination of wire, insulators, a feed line, connectors, and miscellaneous supplies depending on the intended build.

The dipole transfers maximum power when the transmission-line has an impedance congruent with that of the antenna. **Impedance** refers to the amount of electrical resistance to a current as measured in **Ohms**. There are many other types of antenna structures used for amateur radio, including base station J-poles, ground plane antennas, and Yagi antennas.

Since the direction and angle of transmission depends on a its origination point, the height of any antenna has a dramatic effect on radio wave propagation and available communication distances. Higher antenna structures generally reduce the possibility of interference as waves propagate through the **ionosphere,** the ionized layer of the earth's atmosphere through which HF radio waves travel. Consequently, taller antennas require less transmitted power overall.

With these principles in mind, radio enthusiasts may feel tempted to construct extraordinarily tall antennas to expand their communication possibilities. However, both the FCC and **Federal Aviation Administration (FAA)** stipulate that amateur radio operators must stay within legal limits when erecting antenna structures.

Regulations for antennas are largely designed to protect air traffic from unexpectedly encountering radio transmission structures. For antennas not in the vicinity of a public or military airport, structures

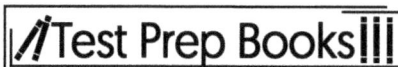

must have a maximum above ground height of 200 feet. For antennas higher than 200 feet or for antennas near the airport, the user must notify the FAA and register with the FCC because there are special restrictions. Notification and registration ensure taller structures' addition to aviation navigational charts, so air traffic controllers and pilots receive accurate information regarding the minimum safe altitude for flight.

The FAA has additional regulations for radio stations within 20,000 feet, or 3.79 miles, of an airport. To determine such limits, the FAA calculates a maximum height dependent on the structure's distance from the nearest airport runway as well as the runway's length. These maximum values can be visualized as an imaginary line with a positive slope, meaning the height limit increases proportionally with increasing distance from the runway.

For example, if the structure is within 20,000 feet from the edge of the nearest runway and the runway is longer than 3,200 feet, then the ratio of the slope dictating maximum structure height is 100:1. When the runway is shorter than 3,200 feet, the regulations require a slope of 50:1 for structures within 10,000 feet.

Finally, local governments do have some control over amateur radio antenna construction. However, they must accommodate amateur radio services and can only include restrictive provisions that do not unreasonably hinder communications. Additionally, state, or local, governments must justify any local regulations with legitimate need.

Good Engineering and Good Amateur Practice

The FCC sets and enforces standards for engineering and amateur radio protocol in the United States. Standards related to amateur radio operations are published in Part 97, which is included in the **Code of Federal Regulations (CFR)** under **Title 47**.

Part 97 was written to establish the purpose and guiding principles for amateur radio users. As stated by the FCC, provisions facilitate the advancement of ham radio communication, strengthen the value of voluntary amateur radio operations for emergency communications, and improve the articulation of radio as a technical art. Part 97 has six parts:

A. General Provisions
B. Station Operating Standards
C. Special Operations
D. Technical Standards
E. Emergency Communications
F. Qualifying Examination Systems

It also includes two appendices which delineate the geographical areas where the FCC regulates amateur radio operation and list volunteer exam coordinator (VEC) regions. These categories cover a wide range of standards, including licensing protocol, equipment regulations, third-party communications, repeater operating conventions, frequency allocations, and emergency radio protocol.

Amateur radio operators must abide by good engineering and amateur practice, as defined under Part 97. However, some instances may arise in which a user exhibits contentious behavior not covered under the FCC's standards for good practice. In such cases, US amateur radio operators can submit a complaint or concern via the FCC's online complaint filing system. Ultimately, ham operators must defer to FCC judgments regarding acceptable praxis.

Subelement G1 – Commission's Rules

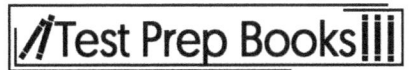

Generally, good amateur practice entails making sure the frequency and mode are permitted by your license class, transmitting via widely accepted band plans, and monitoring chosen frequencies (listening) prior to initiating transmission.

Beacon Operation

A **radio propagation beacon** is a special amateur radio service that transmits a continuous signal to enable observation and assessment of frequency bands. They help ham radio operators determine if their transmissions are likely to successfully contact other operators on a particular band in a certain region of the world. Beacons are also commonly used to analyze propagation.

The **International Beacon Project (IBP)** operates an international network comprised of 18 continuous wave (CW) beacons. The beacons' transmission sites span the globe and are operated by two different volunteer organizations – the **Northern California DX Foundation (NCDXF)** and the **International Amateur Radio Union (IARU)**.

The beacon network is broadcasted in Morse code on a ten-second rotating schedule. Each organization opens their turn transmitting by self-identifying at 100 watts, then proceeds to send dashes at 10 watts, 1 watt, and 100 milliwatts (1/10 watt) respectively. If an amateur radio operator can hear the beacon, it means they can communicate on that frequency with services in the desired region.

Like the IBP beacons, many homemade beacons transmit using **continuous waveforms (CW)**. However, digital beacon systems have become more popular. The **Weak Signal Propagation Reporter**, also known as WSPR, offers one such alternative. **WSPR** is computer software that operates as a digital low-power beacon. It can facilitate communication between amateur radio users, check propagation for both MF and HF bands, and generate reception reports that automatically upload to an online activity database.

The FCC establishes regulations for beacon operation. For example, only one beacon signal can be transmitted at a time in the same band from the same location. The beacon station power limit must be set to 100 watts. Finally, for frequencies 28.20 MHz to 28.30 MHz, automatically controlled beacons are allowed. Automatic beacons are also permitted on other bands for specific frequency ranges, those generally in the middle. However, operators cannot open unattended beacons on any frequency bands below 10m.

Prohibited Transmissions

Part 97 details prohibitions for amateur service transmissions in section 97.113. Amateur radio operators may not communicate with intent to solicit material compensation or fulfill monetary interests. This includes communicating with an employer, except in emergency situations or for the purpose of testing disaster preparation protocols. There are also exceptions for control operators infrequently selling amateur radio equipment, receiving compensation for a ham radio-related teaching job, or sending full-time telegraphy practice transmissions or information bulletins distributed across at least six frequency bands.
Broadcasting, or one-way radio transmission, is strictly prohibited since ham radio is designed for two-way amateur communications and there are other mediums available for broadcasts or one-way programs. However, one-way transmissions are allowed to help with International Morse code learning efforts. For example, users are allowed to broadcast sessions to practice code. Additionally, operators may broadcast relevant communications to preserve human life or secure property in emergency situations.

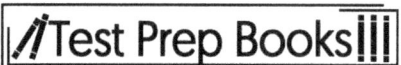

Amateur radio operators cannot use ham frequency bands to carry out criminal activity or intercept radio transmissions for personal gain. Secret codes are not permitted. Since songs could be used as a code or cipher, radio operators cannot broadcast music via voice transmissions. Certain abbreviations are allowed because they are common knowledge in the radio transmission community. However, unfamiliar abbreviations are illegal. The most important component of determining if an abbreviation or signal is allowed is whether it obfuscates the message's meaning.

The ITU itself does not prohibit amateur radio communications anywhere in the world. However, a country can expressly object to amateur radio for communication by its own citizens, in which case the ITU will disallow radio engagement with that state's residents. For example, North Korea and Yemen forbid amateur radio transmissions and, thus, do not issue amateur radio licenses. Therefore, the ITU bans attempts to initiate contact with or responses to received communications from either country.

Retransmitting Radio Signals

Repeaters are devices that can retransmit weak radio signals at a higher power level to boost the signal's range. When a repeater receives a signal on the airwaves, it automatically retransmits the communication. Typically, repeaters allow amateur radio operators to successfully contact services in locations that would be unreachable with a single transmitter.

Ham radio users typically employ FM repeaters to achieve retransmission. An **FM repeater** uses frequency pairs – one frequency receives signals (the listen frequency), while the other retransmits the reception (the talk frequency). Operators usually offset the two frequencies by a standard, recommended value depending on their chosen frequency band. They can simplify this operation by programming their radio with a **transceiver channel**, also known as a **memory channel**, that automatically changes the frequency of transmission when the user either presses or releases their push-to-talk functionality.

Institutions and public safety entities often install repeaters in high altitude locations. However, individual ham users also commonly operate repeaters. Sometimes, amateur radio operators link several repeaters together to create a broader retransmission network. While amateur radio operators can retransmit communication from other amateur stations, they cannot set up a station to do it automatically. Exceptions exist for auxiliary, repeater, and space stations.

Ham operators cannot retransmit broadcast signals from non-amateur stations. In special circumstances, however, the FCC makes exceptions for weather and propagation forecasts from US government stations. Control operators may also retransmit communications from a manned spacecraft if they request and receive approval from the National Aeronautics and Space Administration (NASA). All retransmission exceptions are only allowed as incidental occurrences during regular amateur radio communications.

G1C

Transmitter Power Regulations

The FCC sets strict limits for power usage during amateur radio transmissions. The basic rule stipulates that ham users can only transmit with the minimum power necessary to achieve the desired contact on amateur radio frequency bands.

Subelement G1 – Commission's Rules

Peak Envelope Power (PEP) is the measurement the FCC uses to determine the maximum power usage allowed for radio transmissions. PEP is defined as the maximum average power transmitter during a single frequency cycle. It can also be articulated as the resistive load of transmission. Amateur radio users typically measure PEP with a simple power meter designed to do so.

A more complex way to get an accurate PEP reading requires an oscilloscope, dummy load, and a 2-tone audio generator. An **oscilloscope** is a piece of digital equipment that visualizes voltage signals as waves. A **dummy load** is an electronic device that mimics the electrical resistance of an antenna to help operators test their transmitters prior to going on-air. The electrical resistance produced by the dummy load is expressed in Ohms.

Mathematically, the PEP derives from the **root mean square (rms)** value of the waveform's voltage, measured crest to crest. To find PEP for a transmission, an operator programs the 2-tone audio generator to different, non-harmonious tones with matching amplitudes. They can then measure the voltage between the peaks of the audio waveforms. Finally, the user can calculate PEP by squaring the rms value then dividing the product by the dummy load value. The formula is written as follows:

$$PEP = V_{RMS}^2/R$$

For almost all frequency bands, the maximum power limit is set to 1,500 Watts. For the General license exam, test-takers should remember that 1,500 Watts is the limit for the 12m, 28 MHz, and 1.8 MHz bands. Currently, different power restrictions only apply to the 10.140 MHz, 30m, and 60m bands. For the 10.140 MHz band, the FCC limits the maximum power to 200 Watts. The 60m band has more complex restrictions and is discussed later in this section. The 30m band is designated for sharing; therefore, the FCC limits transmissions to CW and data sent at a 200-Watt maximum power limit.

If an amateur radio operator wishes to communicate on 2200m or 630m bands, they must complete online registration with the **Utilities Technology Council (UTC)**. The UTC is a trade association that manages various utilities and telecommunications infrastructure. Ham users must register in the UTC amateur notification database to ensure communications on the specified bands do not interfere with **power line carriers (PLCs)**. After registration, they must not transmit on the 2200m or 630m bands when operating within 1km (measured horizontally) of a PLC signal.

Data Emission Standards

The FCC also regulates data emission standards. **Data emissions** are measured by the **symbol rate**, or the number of symbol transmissions occurring per second. It can also be defined as bits per second. **Baud**, typically written as **Bd**, is the unit of measurement for symbol rate.

In Part 97, data emission standards appear under section 97.307. Regulations state that amateur radio operators cannot transmit data of a greater bandwidth than necessary. Frequency modulations that produce emissions must not interfere with nearby frequencies. The section also determines the legality for issues related to spurious emissions. A **spurious emission** is data included in a radio transmission that could be omitted without threatening the quality of communication, like when part of a signal is transmitted outside of the intended frequency.

Section 97.307 also includes regulations for data emissions produced via digital signals and **radioteletype (RTTY)**. Simply put, RTTY enables the transmission and reception of printed telegraphy via radio signals carrying messages rendered in Baudot code. The **Baudot code**, which expresses letters,

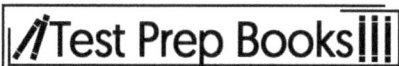

numbers, and punctuation in 5-bit data code, is the language of RTTY. Operators connect a teleprinter to a **RTTY demodulator**, which converts received radio signals to decoded printable data.

In accordance with regulations for prohibited transmissions, operators cannot obfuscate the meaning of a transmission. Therefore, all digital data transmissions must have a publicly documented reference record that includes the code's attributes and the key necessary to decipher encoded messages.

The speed of the symbol transmission rate determines the width of digital and RTTY data signals. A faster transmission rate corresponds with a wider signal. Data emissions standards ensure that transmission signals never become too broad by controlling the acceptable symbol rate. For example, on HF bands, the FCC sets the maximum symbol rate low to avoid overly wide data emissions.

The General class license exam pool includes questions requiring knowledge of the following maximum symbol rates:

- 20m band – 300 baud
- 28 MHz band – 300 baud
- 10m band – 1200 baud
- 2m band – 19.6 kilobaud
- 1.25m band – 56 kilobaud
- 70cm – 56 kilobaud

60-Meter Operation Requirements

Introduced in the early 2000s, the **60m (5 MHz) band** is one of the newest frequency ranges allocated for amateur use. Initially, securing allocation privileges for ham operators on 60m incited controversy between the **National Telecommunications and Information Agency (NTIA)** and the FCC. The NTIA is responsible for administering government use of the radio spectrum, including communications by federal maritime, aviation, private land mobile, and other unspecified users. The agency opposed amateur radio use on the 60m band because it wanted to maintain full control over the band as a matter of homeland security. Ultimately, the FCC negotiated a compromise with the NTIA that allows amateur operators to transmit on five scarcely used, shared channels on the 60m band.

Because of the controversy surrounding amateur radio allocations on 60m, the FCC has imposed strict regulations for transmission. Only hams with General, Advanced, and Amateur Extra licenses can transmit on 60m. As negotiated with the NTIA, amateurs do not have a full band segment allocated to them. Instead, they operate on five discrete channels, or shared spectrum ranges. These channelized portions of the band are available to amateurs on a secondary basis since government agencies use frequencies around these channels. The shared frequencies are **domestic allocations**, meaning they are not available to amateur radio operators internationally. Because privileges are limited, 60m works best for shorter transmissions.

The 60m band allows three operating modes for amateur radio services: upper sideband (USB), continuous wave (CW), and digital modes such as RTTY, PSK31, and PACTOR III. **USB** is the most common communication method used on 60m and refers to a single sideband (SSB) mode of voice transmission. **Single sideband (SSB)** means audio travels via only one part of a modulated waveform that is either above or below the carrier frequency, or basic signal. SSB can propagate over longer distances and generally degrades more slowly and elegantly than **frequency modulation (FM)** or traditional **amplitude modulation (AM)** signals.

Subelement G1 – Commission's Rules

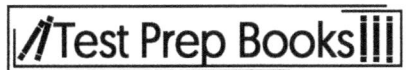

To achieve SSB communication, a **band pass filter** eliminates the unused sideband and the carrier frequency, transmitting only the remaining sideband. SSB effectively limits audio transmissions to either the upper sideband (USB) or **lower sideband (LSB)**. USB is used on shortwave bands, which makes it a perfect mode for 60m phone transmissions.

Bandwidth is the maximum rate data is sent; it measures the speed of data transfer, or a network's capacity, in **bits per second (bps)**. In analogue media, bandwidth refers more specifically to the range of frequencies (the width of the signal) able to be transmitted without losing strength. Bandwidth is measured in in **Hertz (Hz)** and can be calculated by subtracting the lower frequency from the upper frequency. On the 60m band, RTTY signals must have a bandwidth lower than 60Hz.

The **central frequencies** of allocated ranges for hams on 60m include 5332 kHz, 5348 kHz, 5358.5 kHz, 5373 kHz, and 5405 kHz. These are the **suppressed carrier frequencies**, meaning the frequencies shown on a transceiver's display when operating on USB. Since SSB transmissions have a bandwidth of 2.8 kHz, amateur radio operators must transmit within 2.8 kHz wide of any of the channel center frequencies.

Effective Radiated Power (ERP) measures directional RF power, which is the combined power of the antenna gain and the transmitter output. It can also be calculated by multiplying the PEP and the gain. The FCC limits power to 100 watts PEP in relation to a half-wave dipole (100 Watts ERP). If using another type of antenna, the FCC requires operators to keep a record of the antenna gain data to prove they are transmitting within power requirements. Usually this means adding a copy of the manufacturer's published gain specifications in the station records to demonstrate FCC compliance.

Many pieces of amateur radio equipment were not originally created to operate on 60m, so it's likely that operators will need to modify existing hardware to communicate on the band. It is common to upgrade transceivers and alter existing rigs. Additionally, people often make their own antennas to gain access to the 60m band.

Antenna gain refers to the ratio of an antenna's maximum directional signal strength relative to that of a standard antenna. Usually, the referenced standard antenna is either a half-wave dipole or isotropic antenna. An **isotropic antenna** is a theoretical structure with uniform omnidirectional radiation. The gain for a half-wave dipole relative to itself as a standard antenna is 0 decibels (dB). Therefore, it is prohibited to run 100 Watts to an antenna with a higher gain than a half-wave dipole.

One signal is allowed at a time on any given 60m channel. Users need to take care not to overmodulate, so they don't go outside of the designated frequencies. For this reason, older equipment may not be suitable for 60m transmissions. When searching for an open channel, USB operators should search for an open channel by descending from channel 5 to 1; CW and digital users should ascend from 1 to 5. When the user locates an open frequency within the channelized ranges, they may begin transmitting. However, if a primary service interferes, the amateur operator should immediately leave the channel.

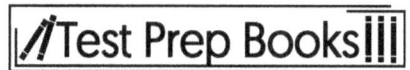

G1D

Volunteer Examiners and Volunteer Examiner Coordinators

The **Amateur Radio Relay League (ARRL)** is the largest licensing organization with an exam system run by volunteers. The **Goldwater-Wirth Bill**, passed in 1982, instituted the Volunteer Examiner Coordinator (VEC) system to administer testing for amateur radio operators. However, the FCC did not officially implement the program until 1984. The **Volunteer Examiner Coordinator (VEC)** refers to an organization comprised of many individual **Volunteer Examiners (VEs)** that organize and manage FCC amateur radio licensing exams. Since the VEC program's inception, more than 50,000 ham radio operators have been accredited to give examinations. The FCC still maintains authority over licensing exams, however, and can choose to offer exams or retest opportunities at any time.

Region	States or Areas Included
1	Connecticut, Maine, Massachusetts, New Hampshire, Rhode Island, and Vermont
2	New Jersey and New York
3	Delaware, District of Columbia, Maryland, and Pennsylvania
4	Alabama, Florida, Georgia, Kentucky, North Carolina, South Carolina, Tennessee, and Virginia
5	Arkansas, Louisiana, Mississippi, New Mexico, Oklahoma, and Texas
6	California
7	Arizona, Idaho, Montana, Nevada, Oregon, Utah, Washington, and Wyoming
8	Michigan, Ohio, and West Virginia
9	Illinois, Indiana, and Wisconsin
10	Colorado, Iowa, Kansas, Minnesota, Missouri, Nebraska, North Dakota, and South Dakota
11	Alaska
12	Caribbean Insular areas
13	Hawaii and Pacific Insular areas

The stated purpose of the VEC is "to provide initial licensing examination for prospective new hams and upgrade examination opportunities for those already licensed." The VEC achieves this purpose primarily by providing ample opportunities for applicants to schedule their licensing exams. Additionally, VEs develop the question pools for licensing exams, so the organization must ensure the test fulfills FCC requirements and adequately assesses familiarity with amateur radio rules and regulations. The VEC audits information received from VEs, ensures there are no discrepancies, and sends required data to the FCC. The organization makes sure VE certifications are completed correctly. Finally, the VEC is committed to ethically fulfilling its mission while providing superior service to all VEs.

Subelement G1 – Commission's Rules

VEs can only administer exams for license classes lower than their own. However, this rule does not apply for the Amateur Extra class examination since there are no more advanced licenses available. VEs with a General class license may give tests to those seeking a Technician license but not those applying for a General license. To protect fairness and consistency in the licensing process, the FCC requires the presence of at least three VEs to give an amateur radio exam, and all VEs must have the correct license for the given test. They are allowed to offer exams at any approved exam administration location.

VEs coordinate and administer three different exams, called exam elements, which include **Element 2 (Technician Class)**, **Element 3 (General Class)**, and **Element 4 (Amateur Extra Class)**.

To administer an amateur radio exam, a VE must be accredited by a VEC and meet the licensing requirements needed to give the exam. Anyone can become a VE if they meet the age and licensing requirements. US citizenship is not a prerequisite. To become a VE, an individual must be at least 18 years old. There are VECs across the country, and all of them can accredit individual VEs. It is simple to become a VE. Interested hams can read the **Volunteer Examiner Manual** online, then submit a VE application form to vec@arrl.org. There are 13 VEC regions under the purview of the FCC. After accreditation, VEs may coordinate exams in one or more of the following areas:

Temporary Identification

A **Certificate of Successful Completion (CSCE)** is issued to every candidate that passes their licensing exam. The CSCE remains valid for the following 365 days. The VEs send all CSCEs to the FCC straightaway, so that all new operators can immediately begin transmitting on channels available to their licensing class. It generally takes about one week for the FCC to update a candidate's status in its database. While waiting for the upgrade to appear on the FCC's webpage, individuals who have passed the General licensing exam can add the abbreviation "AG" to their callsign. **AG** stands for **Awaiting General**. Using this abbreviation, Technician class operators with a General class CSCE can operate on any band segment available to General or Technician class license-holding individuals.

Element Credit

When amateur radio licenses expire, operators have a grace period of two years during which they can renew their license. However, for amateurs that have previously held a General class license or higher, the VEC offers individuals an opportunity to reinstate their expired license even after the grace period has ended. This option allows hams to regain their earned license class by 1) proving that they have obtained a General, Advanced, or Amateur Extra license in the past and 2) passing the Technician class test (Element 2). Additionally, the VEC has the authority to grant **partial element credit** for expired licenses. Anyone who previously held a valid license can earn a portion of credit toward reinstating their class. However, element credit is not available for prior operators who have had their license revoked by the FCC. This program functions via local VEC organizations, so interested individuals should contact their nearest group of VEs for further information.

G1E

Control Categories

A **control operator** monitors radio transmissions from an amateur station to ensure FCC compliance. The designated control operator bears the responsibility for any transmissions sent from their station.

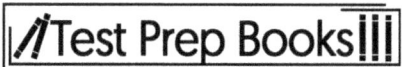

Subelement G1 – Commission's Rules

Every amateur radio station must have a control operator. However, they do not always have to physically observe the transmitter. Usually, the license-holding individual is the designated control operator. Because the Technician exam largely covers content related to control operators, the General exam only has two potential queries included in the question pool.

The first possible question addresses circumstances in which the control operator must manage the threat of harmful interference. According to the ARRL, **harmful interference** includes emissions, radiation, or induction that jeopardizes radio navigation, impedes emergency services, or frequently disrupts communication for radio users or infrastructure. There are certain conditions that require control operators to follow specific protocols to reduce the likelihood of harmful interference. These situations include transmitting within one mile of an FCC Monitoring Station, operating on a shared band, and spreading spectrum emissions across a greater range of bandwidth. In each of these cases, the control operator must exercise caution to prevent difficulties during transmission.

Spread spectrum transmissions, also known as **frequency hopping**, helps control operators avoid harmful interference. Spread spectrum distributes radio signals across a broader section of bandwidth, making transmissions more resilient when they encounter any kind of interference. The FCC sets strict power limits for spread spectrum communications; control operators cannot exceed 10 watts of PEP output. Part 97 regulations remain applicable for all digital transmissions regardless of intentional or unintentional frequency interference. Operators should remember that the **International Beacon Project (IBP)** uses 14.100, 18.110, 21.150, 24.930, and 28.200 MHz for its propagation beacons. Therefore, hams should steer clear of these frequencies when communicating using spread spectrum transmissions.

2.4 GHz, or 13cm, is a shared band on the microwave radio spectrum. It is one of several bands designated primarily for **industrial, scientific, and medical (ISM)** purposes. This means amateur radio operators are secondary on 2.4. ISM includes a broad range of services and devices including Bluetooth, microwave ovens, and mobile cellular services. Additionally, 2.4 GHz is commonly used as a wireless networking frequency, which means hams transmitting on its channels must share bandwidth with unlicensed Wi-Fi services. Unlicensed wireless networks can function as **Amateur Radio Emergency Data Networks (AREDNs)** for communicating between licensed stations. However, control operators should note that they may not correspond with unlicensed stations. Finally, they are likely to encounter significant harmful interference while using this band because of ISM-related crowding.

Repeater Regulations

Earning a General class license expands an amateur radio operator's repeater privileges. While those with Technician class licenses may use the 10m band, they may not operate in the repeater section of the band. Hams must hold a General class license to retransmit a signal with a 10m repeater. However, they can use 10m repeaters to retransmit signals sent on the 2m band by a control operator with a Technician class license.

Third-Party Rules

Third-party traffic refers to situations where unlicensed individuals communicate on amateur stations. While permitted in the United States, control operators should understand that some countries ban third-party traffic. The FCC limits the content of third-party transmissions to ham-related messages, personal statement, or emergency communications. Anyone may transmit as a third party if they have not had a previously held amateur radio license revoked, in which case the operator is banned. Therefore, a revoked license must be reinstated by the FCC before the holder can transmit again.

ITU Regions

The **International Telecommunications Union**, or ITU, segments global radio communications into three geographical regions. **Line B** is an important reference that defines the regional boundaries; it runs from the North Pole, beginning at meridian 10 degrees West, to the South Pole, concluding at meridian 20 degrees West. **Region 1** begins east of Line B and includes Europe, Africa, the post-Soviet states, Mongolia, and Middle Eastern countries located west of the Persian Gulf. **Region 2** lies west of Line B and includes the Americas and some Pacific Islands. Finally, **Region 3** includes all remaining states, including most Asian countries outside of the Former Soviet Union (FSU) and the majority of Oceania. ITU sets various frequency allocations for all geographical regions outside of ITU Region 2. Since Region 2 largely comprises the Americas, the FCC has significant jurisdiction over its frequency allocations. Therefore, amateur operators in North or South America should conduct themselves according to FCC regulations and transmit using Region 2 frequency allocations.

Automatically Controlled Digital Station

There are three forms of digital station control mechanisms: automatic, local, or remote. An **automatically controlled digital station (ACDS)** refers to a digital station that can transmit messages without an operator present. These types of stations utilize internet capabilities to automatically transfer and receive radio signals. Specific band segments, called limited segments, are allocated for ACDSs since they cannot listen and adjust for interference. For example, within bandwidths 6m or below and in designated HF bands, ACDSs may communicate with one another via RTTY or data emissions. If an operator receives a digital transmission outside of the channels allocated for automatic transmission, then they can presume the original station operates under either local or remote control.

Subelement G1 – Questions

G1A

1. On which HF and/or MF amateur bands are there portions where General class licensees cannot transmit?
    a. 60 meters, 30 meters, 17 meters, and 12 meters
    b. 160 meters, 60 meters, 15 meters, and 12 meters
    c. 80 meters, 40 meters, 20 meters, and 15 meters
    d. 80 meters, 20 meters, 15 meters, and 10 meters

2. On which of the following bands is phone operation prohibited?
    a. 160 meters
    b. 30 meters
    c. 17 meters
    d. 12 meters

3. On which of the following bands is image transmission prohibited?
    a. 160 meters
    b. 30 meters
    c. 20 meters
    d. 12 meters

4. Which of the following amateur bands is restricted to communication only on specific channels, rather than frequency ranges?
    a. 11 meters
    b. 12 meters
    c. 30 meters
    d. 60 meters

5. On which of the following frequencies are General class licensees prohibited from operating as control operator?
    a. 7.125 MHz to 7.175 MHz
    b. 28.000 MHz to 28.025 MHz
    c. 21.275 MHz to 21.300 MHz
    d. All of the above

6. Which of the following applies when the FCC rules designate the amateur service as a secondary user on a band?
    a. Amateur stations must record the call sign of the primary service station before operating on a frequency assigned to that station
    b. Amateur stations may use the band only during emergencies
    c. Amateur stations must not cause harmful interference to primary users and must accept interference from primary users
    d. Amateur stations may only operate during specific hours of the day, while primary users are permitted 24-hour use of the band

Subelement G1 – Commission's Rules

7. On which amateur frequencies in the 10-meter band may stations with a General class control operator transmit CW emissions?
   a. 28.000 MHz to 28.025 MHz only
   b. 28.000 MHz to 28.300 MHz only
   c. 28.025 MHz to 28.300 MHz only
   d. The entire band

8. Which HF bands have segments exclusively allocated to Amateur Extra licensees?
   a. All HF bands
   b. 80 meters, 40 meters, 20 meters, and 15 meters
   c. All HF bands except 160 meters and 10 meters
   d. 60 meters, 30 meters, 17 meters, and 12 meters

9. Which of the following frequencies is within the General class portion of the 15-meter band?
   a. 14250 kHz
   b. 18155 kHz
   c. 21300 kHz
   d. 24900 kHz

10. What portion of the 10-meter band is available for repeater use?
    a. The entire band
    b. The portion between 28.1 MHz and 28.2 MHz
    c. The portion between 28.3 MHz and 28.5 MHz
    d. The portion above 29.5 MHz

11. When General class licensees are not permitted to use the entire voice portion of a band, which portion of the voice segment is available to them?
    a. The lower frequency portion
    b. The upper frequency portion
    c. The lower frequency portion on frequencies below 7.3 MHz, and the upper portion on frequencies above 14.150 MHz
    d. The upper frequency portion on frequencies below 7.3 MHz, and the lower portion on frequencies above 14.150 MHz

G1B

1. What is the maximum height above ground for an antenna structure not near a public use airport without requiring notification to the FAA and registration with the FCC?
   a. 50 feet
   b. 100 feet
   c. 200 feet
   d. 250 feet

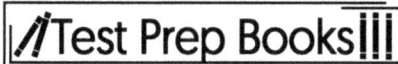

2. With which of the following conditions must beacon stations comply?
   a. No more than one beacon station may transmit in the same band from the same station location
   b. The frequency must be coordinated with the National Beacon Organization
   c. The frequency must be posted on the internet or published in a national periodical
   d. All these choices are correct

3. Which of the following is a purpose of a beacon station as identified in the FCC rules?
   a. Observation of propagation and reception
   b. Automatic identification of repeaters
   c. Transmission of bulletins of general interest to amateur radio licensees
   d. All these choices are correct

4. Which of the following transmissions is permitted for all amateur stations?
   a. Unidentified transmissions of less than 10 seconds duration for test purposes only
   b. Automatic retransmission of other amateur signals by any amateur station
   c. Occasional retransmission of weather and propagation forecast information from US government stations
   d. Encrypted messages, if not intended to facilitate a criminal act

5. Which of the following one-way transmissions are permitted?
   a. Unidentified test transmissions of less than 10 seconds in duration
   b. Transmissions to assist with learning the International Morse code
   c. Regular transmissions offering equipment for sale, if intended for amateur radio use
   d. All these choices are correct

6. Under what conditions are state and local governments permitted to regulate amateur radio antenna structures?
   a. Under no circumstances, FCC rules take priority
   b. At any time and to any extent necessary to accomplish a legitimate purpose of the state or local entity, provided that proper filings are made with the FCC
   c. Only when such structures exceed 50 feet in height and are clearly visible 1,000 feet from the structure
   d. Amateur Service communications must be reasonably accommodated, and regulations must constitute the minimum practical to accommodate a legitimate purpose of the state or local entity

7. What are the restrictions on the use of abbreviations or procedural signals in the amateur service?
   a. Only "Q" signals are permitted
   b. They may be used if they do not obscure the meaning of a message
   c. They are not permitted
   d. They are limited to those expressly listed in Part 97 of the FCC rules

Subelement G1 – Commission's Rules

8. When is it permissible to communicate with amateur stations in countries outside the areas administered by the Federal Communications Commission?
    a. Only when the foreign country has a formal third-party agreement filed with the FCC
    b. When the contact is with amateurs in any country except those whose administrations have notified the ITU that they object to such communications
    c. Only when the contact is with amateurs licensed by a country which is a member of the United Nations, or by a territory possessed by such a country
    d. Only when the contact is with amateurs licensed by a country which is a member of the International Amateur Radio Union, or by a territory possessed by such a country

9. On what HF frequencies are automatically controlled beacons permitted?
    a. On any frequency if power is less than 1 watt
    b. On any frequency if transmissions are in Morse code
    c. 21.08 MHz to 21.09 MHz
    d. 28.20 MHz to 28.30 MHz

10. What is the power limit for beacon stations?
    a. 10 watts PEP output
    b. 20 watts PEP output
    c. 100 watts PEP output
    d. 200 watts PEP output

11. Who or what determines "good engineering and good amateur practice," as applied to the operation of an amateur station in all respects not covered by the Part 97 rules?
    a. The FCC
    b. The control operator
    c. The IEEE
    d. The ITU

G1C

1. What is the maximum transmitter power an amateur station may use on 10.140 MHz?
    a. 200 watts PEP output
    b. 1000 watts PEP output
    c. 1500 watts PEP output
    d. 2000 watts PEP output

2. What is the maximum transmitter power an amateur station may use on the 12-meter band?
    a. 50 watts PEP output
    b. 200 watts PEP output
    c. 1500 watts PEP output
    d. An effective radiated power equivalent to 100 watts from a half-wave dipole

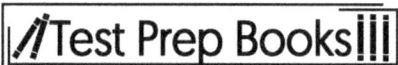

Subelement G1 – Commission's Rules

3. What is the maximum bandwidth permitted by FCC rules for amateur radio stations transmitting on USB frequencies in the 60-meter band?
   a. 2.8 kHz
   b. 5.6 kHz
   c. 1.8 kHz
   d. 3 kHz

4. Which of the following is required by the FCC rules when operating in the 60-meter band?
   a. You must keep a record of the gain of your antenna if you are using an antenna other than a dipole
   b. You must keep a record of the date, time, frequency, power level, and stations worked
   c. You must keep a record of all third-party traffic
   d. You must keep a record of the manufacturer of your equipment and the antenna used

5. What is the limit for transmitter power on the 28 MHz band for a General Class control operator?
   a. 100 watts PEP output
   b. 1000 watts PEP output
   c. 1500 watts PEP output
   d. 2000 watts PEP output

6. What is the limit for transmitter power on the 1.8 MHz band?
   a. 200 watts PEP output
   b. 1000 watts PEP output
   c. 1200 watts PEP output
   d. 1500 watts PEP output

7. What must be done before using a new digital protocol on the air?
   a. Type-certify equipment to FCC standards
   b. Obtain an experimental license from the FCC
   c. Publicly document the technical characteristics of the protocol
   d. Submit a rule-making proposal to the FCC describing the codes and methods of the technique

8. What is the maximum symbol rate permitted for RTTY or data emission transmitted at frequencies below 28 MHz?
   a. 56 kilobaud
   b. 19.6 kilobaud
   c. 1200 baud
   d. 300 baud

9. What is the maximum power limit on the 60-meter band?
   a. 1500 watts PEP
   b. 10 watts RMS
   c. ERP of 100 watts PEP with respect to a dipole
   d. ERP of 100 watts PEP with respect to an isotropic antenna

Subelement G1 – Commission's Rules

10. What is the maximum symbol rate permitted for RTTY or data emission transmissions on the 10-meter band?
    a. 56 kilobaud
    b. 19.6 kilobaud
    c. 1200 baud
    d. 300 baud

11. What measurement is specified by FCC rules that regulate maximum power?
    a. RMS output from the transmitter
    b. RMS input to the antenna
    c. PEP input to the antenna
    d. PEP output from the transmitter

G1D

1. Who may receive partial credit for the elements represented by an expired amateur radio license?
    a. Any person who can demonstrate that they once held an FCC-issued General, Advanced, or Amateur Extra class license that was not revoked by the FCC
    b. Anyone who held an FCC-issued amateur radio license that expired not less than 5 and not more than 15 years ago
    c. Any person who previously held an amateur license issued by another country, but only if that country has a current reciprocal licensing agreement with the FCC
    d. Only persons who once held an FCC issued Novice, Technician, or Technician Plus license

2. What license examinations may you administer as an accredited Volunteer Examiner holding a General class operator license?
    a. General and Technician
    b. None, only Amateur Extra class licensees may be accredited
    c. Technician only
    d. Amateur Extra, General, and Technician

3. On which of the following band segments may you operate if you are a Technician class operator and have an unexpired Certificate of Successful Completion of Examination (CSCE) for General class privileges?
    a. Only the Technician band segments until your upgrade is posted in the FCC database
    b. Only on the Technician band segments until you have a receipt for the FCC application fee payment
    c. On any General or Technician class band segment
    d. On any General or Technician class band segment except 30 meters and 60 meters

4. Who must observe the administration of a Technician class license examination?
    a. At least three Volunteer Examiners of General class or higher
    b. At least two Volunteer Examiners of General class or higher
    c. At least two Volunteer Examiners of Technician class or higher
    d. At least three Volunteer Examiners of Technician class

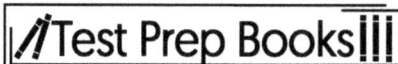

Subelement G1 – Commission's Rules

5. When operating a US station by remote control from outside the country, what license is required of the control operator?
   a. A US operator/primary station license
   b. Only an appropriate US operator/primary license and a special remote station permit from the FCC
   c. Only a license from the foreign country, as long as the call sign includes identification of portable operation in the US
   d. A license from the foreign country and a special remote station permit from the FCC

6. Until an upgrade to General class is shown in the FCC database, when must a Technician licensee identify with "AG" after their call sign?
   a. Whenever they operate using General class frequency privileges
   b. Whenever they operate on any amateur frequency
   c. Whenever they operate using Technician frequency privileges
   d. A special identifier is not required if their General class license application has been filed with the FCC

7. Volunteer Examiners are accredited by what organization?
   a. The Federal Communications Commission
   b. The Universal Licensing System
   c. A Volunteer Examiner Coordinator
   d. The Wireless Telecommunications Bureau

8. Which of the following criteria must be met for a non-US citizen to be an accredited Volunteer Examiner?
   a. The person must be a resident of the US for a minimum of 5 years
   b. The person must hold an FCC granted amateur radio license of General class or above
   c. The person's home citizenship must be in ITU region 2
   d. None of these choices is correct; a non-US citizen cannot be a Volunteer Examiner

9. How long is a Certificate of Successful Completion of Examination (CSCE) valid for exam element credit?
   a. 30 days
   b. 180 days
   c. 365 days
   d. For as long as your current license is valid

10. What is the minimum age that one must be to qualify as an accredited Volunteer Examiner?
    a. 16 years
    b. 18 years
    c. 21 years
    d. There is no age limit

Subelement G1 – Commission's Rules

11. What action is required to obtain a new General class license after a previously held license has expired and the two-year grace period has passed?
    a. They must have a letter from the FCC showing they once held an amateur or commercial license
    b. There are no requirements other than being able to show a copy of the expired license
    c. Contact the FCC to have the license reinstated
    d. The applicant must show proof of the appropriate expired license grant and pass the current Element 2 exam

12. When operating a station in South America by remote control over the internet from the US, what regulations apply?
    a. Those of both the remote station's country and the FCC
    b. Those of the remote station's country and the FCC's third-party regulations
    c. Only those of the remote station's country
    d. Only those of the FCC

G1E

1. Which of the following would disqualify a third party from participating in sending a message via an amateur station?
    a. The third party's amateur license has been revoked and not reinstated
    b. The third party is not a US citizen
    c. The third party is speaking in a language other than English
    d. All these choices are correct

2. When may a 10-meter repeater retransmit the 2-meter signal from a station that has a Technician class control operator?
    a. Under no circumstances
    b. Only if the station on 10-meters is operating under a Special Temporary Authorization allowing such retransmission
    c. Only during an FCC-declared general state of communications emergency
    d. Only if the 10-meter repeater control operator holds at least a General class license

3. What is required to conduct communications with a digital station operating under automatic control outside the automatic control band segments?
    a. The station initiating the contact must be under local or remote control
    b. The interrogating transmission must be made by another automatically controlled station
    c. No third-party traffic may be transmitted
    d. The control operator of the interrogating station must hold an Amateur Extra class license

4. Which of the following conditions require a licensed amateur radio operator to take specific steps to avoid harmful interference to other users or facilities?
    a. When operating within one mile of an FCC Monitoring Station
    b. When using a band where the Amateur Service is secondary
    c. When a station is transmitting spread spectrum emissions
    d. All these choices are correct

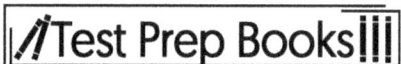

Subelement G1 – Commission's Rules

5. What are the restrictions on messages sent to a third party in a country with which there is a Third-Party Agreement?
    a. They must relate to emergencies or disaster relief
    b. They must be for other licensed amateurs
    c. They must relate to amateur radio, or remarks of a personal character, or messages relating to emergencies or disaster relief
    d. The message must be limited to no longer than 1 minute in duration and the name of the third party must be recorded in the station log

6. The frequency allocations of which ITU region apply to radio amateurs operating in North and South America?
    a. Region 4
    b. Region 3
    c. Region 2
    d. Region 1

7. In what part of the 2.4 GHz band may an amateur station communicate with non-licensed Wi-Fi stations?
    a. Anywhere in the band
    b. Channels 1 through 4
    c. Channels 42 through 45
    d. No part

8. What is the maximum PEP output allowed for spread spectrum transmissions?
    a. 100 milliwatts
    b. 10 watts
    c. 100 watts
    d. 1500 watts

9. Under what circumstances are messages that are sent via digital modes exempt from Part 97 third-party rules that apply to other modes of communication?
    a. Under no circumstances
    b. When messages are encrypted
    c. When messages are not encrypted
    d. When under automatic control

10. Why should an amateur operator normally avoid transmitting on 14.100, 18.110, 21.150, 24.930 and 28.200 MHz?
    a. A system of propagation beacon stations operates on those frequencies
    b. A system of automatic digital stations operates on those frequencies
    c. These frequencies are set aside for emergency operations
    d. These frequencies are set aside for bulletins from the FCC

Subelement G1 – Commission's Rules

11. On what bands may automatically controlled stations transmitting RTTY or data emissions communicate with other automatically controlled digital stations?
    a. On any band segment where digital operation is permitted
    b. Anywhere in the non-phone segments of the 10-meter or shorter wavelength bands
    c. Only in the non-phone Extra Class segments of the bands
    d. Anywhere in the 6-meter or shorter wavelength bands, and in limited segments of some of the HF bands

12. When may third-party messages be transmitted via remote control?
    a. Under any circumstances in which third party messages are permitted by FCC rules
    b. Under no circumstances except for emergencies
    c. Only when the message is intended for licensed radio amateurs
    d. Only when the message is intended for third parties in areas where licensing is controlled by the FCC

Subelement G1 – Answer Key

G1A

1. C	7. D
2. B	8. B
3. B	9. C
4. D	10. D
5. A	11. B
6. C	

G1B

1. C	7. B
2. A	8. B
3. A	9. D
4. C	10. C
5. B	11. A
6. D	

G1C

1. A	7. C
2. C	8. D
3. A	9. C
4. A	10. C
5. C	11. D
6. D	

G1D

1. A	7. C
2. C	8. B
3. C	9. C
4. A	10. B
5. A	11. D
6. A	12. C

G1E

1. A	7. D
2. D	8. B
3. A	9. A
4. D	10. A
5. C	11. D
6. C	12. A

Subelement G2 – Operating Procedures

G2A

Phone Operating Procedures

The ham radio community prides itself on its behavioral standards of consideration, tolerance, kindness, and patience, which are both embedded in amateur radio culture and supported by FCC regulations. Amateur operators are self-correcting, meaning the community mostly polices itself.

Amateur protocol requires users to avoid language native to citizens band radio (CB radio) and adopt ham language. The **Q-code** is an official radiotelegraph communication convention that uses three-letter signals to represent common words or phrases. Amateur radio operators should always use a combination of the Q-code and plain language to communicate during transmission.

Much of amateur radio vocabulary stems from Morse code telegraphy standards. For example, 73 means "best regards" and 88 means "love and kisses." OM means "old man" and is a code used to describe a male operator of any age; and YL, an abbreviation for "young lady," refers to a female operator. However, the term ham comes from a derogatory term used to describe amateur radio operators whose skills were deemed "ham-fisted."

Amateur radio uses the **phonetic alphabet**, also known as the **international aviation or NATO alphabet**, to facilitate transmission of important information under suboptimal conditions. Ham operators should memorize this alphabet so they can communicate crucial messages even while transmitting on noisy or inconsistent frequencies.

International Aviation Alphabet							
A	Alpha	H	Hotel	O	Oscar	V	Victor
B	Bravo	I	India	P	Papa	W	Whiskey
C	Charlie	J	Juliet	Q	Quebec	X	X-Ray
D	Delta	K	Kilo	R	Romeo	Y	Yankee
E	Echo	L	Lima	S	Sierra	Z	Zulu
F	Foxtrot	M	Mike	T	Tango		
G	Golf	N	November	U	Uniform		

If beginning a new QSO, hams should ensure the desired frequency is available before transmitting by asking if the frequency is currently in use. Before initiating communication, ham operators can use a dummy load to tune the transmitter to a specific frequency without generating radio waves. **Dummy loads** imitate an antenna by supplying a simulated electrical load to an audio amplifier. This allows the operator to adjust or "tune" the frequency of their transmissions. During tuning, the amateur radio operator should first ensure that propagation conditions will allow clear transmission for the intended direction and range.

First, radio operators should check Maximum Usable Frequency (MUF) charts to determine the likelihood of successful transmission for specific frequencies according to present ionospheric conditions. Next, hams should read the band plan for their desired frequency range and determine the appropriate frequency for voice transmissions according to FCC allocations.

An **Automatic Level Control (ALC)** is a circuit included on most audio amplifiers that controls power output. It regulates the level of power by imposing parameters on Ohm usage such that the audio amplifier operates with the minimum power necessary to transmit without signal distortion. Essentially, the ALC throttles the electrical load to prevent grid destruction during transmission and ensure efficient usage of frequency bands. To calibrate the ALC circuit to the appropriate setting, operators can adjust the audio transmission or microphone gain.

USB/LSB Conventions

The graphical representation of an Amplitude Modulated (AM) audio signal has two sidebands reflected symmetrically across the axis of the carrier signal. Each sideband is illustrated as an **envelope**, or the outlined curvature of a modulating waveform intended to emphasize the extremes of the instantaneous amplitude of a sine wave. There is an **upper sideband (USB)** above and a **lower sideband (LSB)** below the **carrier signal**, or central frequency.

Because the sidebands carry identical information, transmissions can remove one side of the signal as well as the carrier signal without losing any audio information. When a transmission eliminates one sideband (either the USB or LSB) and the carrier by suppressing the signals, the mode of communication is called **single sideband (SSB)**. SSB is the most common mode of voice transmission used in amateur radio because it conserves power and utilizes less bandwidth.

Good amateur practice conventions dictate whether a radio operator uses LSB or USB transmission. Typically, LSB occurs on lower frequencies, and USB messages transmit on higher frequencies. LSB is customarily used when communicating on the 160m, 75m, and 40m bands. Note that 75m is the portion of the 80m band spectrum allocated for voice transmissions. USB transmissions occur on wavelengths of 14MHz and above, including the 17m and 12m bands. Operators always use USB when transmitting on VHF and UHF bands.

Breaking Into a Contact

Often, ham operators wish to join a discussion already happening on their chosen frequency band. The code **QSO** refers to an ongoing conversation, and there are certain protocols considered "good amateur practice" for interrupting a QSO. Most importantly, operators should listen before joining a QSO, making sure to pay attention to the callsigns of those involved in the ongoing conversation. It's important to wait for the transmission to switch stations before entering, or "breaking in" to the QSO.

To break in, the operator should state their entire callsign once to self-identify and then stand by until the transmitting station acknowledges them. After breaking into contact, operators should address conversation partners by their first name only. Operators should avoid using the term "break" during a transmission since this generally indicates an emergency.

Subelement G2 – Operating Procedures

When making a general solicitation for conversation, ham operators use a CQ call. **CQ** is a code originating from the French word "securité," and often referred to as "seek you" by English speakers. Calling CQ means the operator transmits the code several times in a row on SSB voice mode or CW mode (e.g., "CQ CQ CQ") until another operator responds. The use of repetitive calls consisting of the same letters gives the responding operator a simple auditory basis for fine-tuning their station's transceiver. Other letters can be added to CQ to change the meaning. For example, **CQD** indicates a distress call. In American radio, **CQ DX** means the operator wishes to contact stations outside of the continental US.

Transmitter Setup for Voice Operation

A **voice operated switch**, also known as **voice operated relay** or **voice operated exchange (VOX)**, is an alternative to **Push to Talk (PTT) transmission switches** that relies on the operator's voice to trigger transmission. VOX systems work by detecting the decibel level of environmental sounds and responding to speech that exceeds a certain volume. Automatic, touchless operation is the most obvious advantage to using VOX.

Answering DX Stations

When answering a call from a distant station, it's important to be clear and concise and to make sure the information is understood. If necessary, ask the calling station to repeat their location or ask if you are being called and give your own callsign. When calling another station, address the callsign of the station you're calling and give your own callsign and approximate location. Whenever you read out your callsign, it's also a good idea to speak it using a phonetic alphabet at least once as well, such as reading K9RTZ as Kilo Nine Romeo Tango Zulu.

In some situations, many calls may be incoming to the same stations at once, a possibility sometimes known as a **pileup**. In this case, focus on making individual calls as short as possible—ideally no more than two or three seconds. Keeping calls quick and concise with all the information needed may take some practice, but it's considered good courtesy to avoid making a call any longer than it must be during a pileup.

G2B

Operating Courtesy

All amateur stations have equal access to frequencies allocated for ham usage. Since amateur radio bands are shared between operators, licensed users should remember that frequencies can be used by everyone. Operators should try to avoid interfering with others' transmissions. To check whether a frequency is open, amateurs should transmit the Q-code "QRL?" followed by their call sign on CW, which asks other operators that may be using the frequency if it is available. In voice mode, amateurs can simply ask whether the channel is busy then state their call sign. Additionally, operators must take care to distance themselves from ongoing conversations on nearby frequencies. On CW, amateurs should keep at least 150 – 500 Hz between their transmissions and the next closest QSO; on SSB, operators should keep at least 3 kHz of separation.

Subelement G2 – Operating Procedures

Operators should treat each other with courtesy while still communicating directly; sometimes, a user may ask another to move to a different frequency to avoid crowding or address a transmission issue. However, if an operator already has domain over a certain frequency, they have no legal obligation to move except in an emergency. When property or human life are at stake, operators may interrupt a QSL with intent to take over the channel. In that case, the emergency transmission should receive priority access. If someone breaks in needing assistance for an emergency, operators must respond to the call then listen to ascertain how to help the station in distress.

Since propagation depends on ionospheric conditions, the clarity of an operator's frequency may change suddenly. Sometimes, such changes introduce **interference** into the band. When this happens, operators may cross wires with one another and frequencies may pick up other stations, which can cause crowding on the channel. Solving this issue requires operators to work together as well as independently to remedy the issue in a way that is agreeable to everyone. Amateur radio users should keep in mind that propagation issues can present interesting, complex, and enjoyable challenges, and it is imperative to treat one another politely and respectfully while resolving these problems.

Band Plans

Before beginning to transmit, hams should check the **voluntary band plan** to select a frequency for the desired operating mode. Following the band plan helps amateur radio operators know what to expect from each other's chosen communication modes and frequencies. The General exam requires candidates to know the DX (distance) voluntary band plan for 6m, which allocates 50.1 to 50.125 MHz for contacts outside of the contiguous United States (48 states).

Drills and Emergencies

The **Radio Amateur Civil Emergency Service (RACES)** is a volunteer service enacted by both the **Federal Emergency Management Agency (FEMA)** and the FCC that coordinates ham radio during emergencies. To participate in emergency communications or relief efforts, control operators acting as RACES volunteers must hold an amateur radio license granted by the FCC.

During emergencies, operators may operate outside of usual frequency allocations with higher power outputs. The priority lies in communicating the call for help and assisting those transmitting a distress signal. Operators in distress, or helping those who are, should transmit on any frequency that provides the highest likelihood of reception, regardless of their license class. In short, hams are allowed to do whatever it takes to notify others of an emergency or to support a distressed station.

RACES Operation

The War Powers Act of 1941 gives the President of the United States the authority to suspend the Amateur Radio Service in the event of war. In such an event, services are replaced by the **Radio Amateur Civil Emergency Service (RACES)**, a network of volunteers that register with state, county, and local emergency services to help coordinate response efforts. Since its creation in 1952, it has never been activated, but it is still important for volunteers to train and understand their responsibilities should RACES ever be required.

Licensed amateurs who volunteer must be certified by a civil defense agency such as the Federal Civil Defense Administration and must be able to clearly communicate on amateur radio frequencies during

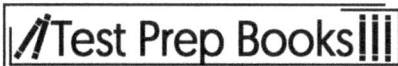

drills and exercises. RACES volunteers should stay up to date on preparedness documentation; more information on such documentation can be found at https://www.usraces.org/.

G2C

CW Operating Procedures and Procedural Signals

Continuous wavelength (CW) mode in ham radio refers to communication using Morse code transmissions. The General exam does not require amateurs to learn Morse code. However, there are certain abbreviations, derived from Morse code telegraphy, that come in handy for all operators. Many of these abbreviations are known as procedure signs.

In CW, a **procedure sign**, or a **prosign**, refers to a combination of letters without spaces used as shorthand in Morse code telegraphy. For example, an operator would use the prosign AR, meaning all remitted, to demarcate the end of a CW transmission. The following chart is a list of commonly used prosigns. Those included in questions on the General exam have a star placed next to them.

When communicating with CW, operators need to coordinate with one another to make sure they are transmitting at a comfortable speed for both parties. Whoever sends the initial CQ sets the expectation for the response speed since they will transmit at an appropriate pace for themselves. When answering a CQ, operators should transmit as quickly as they comfortably can but not faster than the CQ speed. It's crucial that both conversation partners can easily keep up with transmissions.

CW communications require operators to "zero beat" each other. **Zero beat** means adjusting the transmission frequency to exactly match that of the signal received from one's conversation partner. Operators can match the received signal by tuning the CW sidetone. When both operators have tuned to the same frequency, the receive and transmit tones will match up perfectly.

RST refers to a three number coded system that helps operators easily communicate a signal's level of **readability, strength, and tone**. Readability is assessed with the following scale: 1 – Unreadable, 2 – Barely readable, 3 – Readable with significant difficulty, 4 – Readable with almost no difficulty, and 5 – Perfectly readable. Strength and tone are both rated on a scale of 1 to 9, with 1 being the lowest quality and 9 being the highest quality transmission for the respective criteria.

Operators select a rating for each category and combine them into a code with three numbers to alert other stations to the quality of a received transmission. Amateur radio users call this code an **RST report**. For example, an amateur radio user might transmit the code 268 to indicate low readability, good signal strength, and a nearly perfect tone with slight ripples.

When a control station's power supply is not properly regulated, transmissions can become unstable and cause signal chirping. Adding a C to the end of the RST report lets the other station know that the signal has been destabilized and sounds chirpy. For example, an operator may transmit the code 487C.

Q Signals and Common Abbreviations

Q-signals are abbreviations, or **radio shorthand**, that simplify communication between amateur radio operators to increase efficiency, reduce language barriers, and improve the experience and quality of transmissions, Q-signals were originally created to communicate in Morse code and was popularized for voice transmissions, as well.

Subelement G2 – Operating Procedures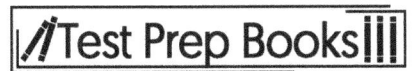

The following table lists the most common Q signals used in amateur radio transmissions as recognized by the ARRL. Rating scales are evaluated using the signifiers 1 through 5 with the following meanings: 1 – nil, 2 – slightly, 3 – moderately, 4 – severely, 5 – extremely. Those Q signals included in questions on the General exam have a star placed next to them.

Abbreviation	Meaning
ADR	Address
ANT	Antenna
AR	All remitted
AS	Wait
BT	Break in text
BK	Break in (invitation)
C*	Confirm, yes
CFM	Confirm
CL	Clear, closing station
CUL	See you later
ES	And
GA	Go ahead or good afternoon
GB	Goodbye
GND	Ground
HI	Laughter
HR	Here or hear
K	Go ahead
KN*	Go ahead (listening for a specific station)
N	No
NIL	Nothing
NR	Number
OM	Old man
OP	Operator

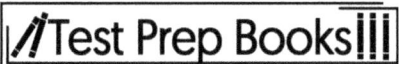

Abbreviation	Meaning
OT	Old timer
PSE	Please
QRL	Is the frequency busy?
R	Roger, yes
RPT	Repeat or report
RX or RCVR	Receiver
SIG	Signal
SK	End of message
SKED	Schedule
SRI	Sorry
TNX	Thanks
TVI	Television interference
TX	Transmitter
VY	Very
WKG	Working
WL	Will
WX	Weather
XMTR	Transmitter
YL	Young lady
73	Best regards
88	Love and kisses

Full Break-In

Full break-in operation (QSK) is a telegraphy operating mode where transceivers can detect other stations' signals in between the dots and dashes or letters of CW coded messages. This happens as the station rapidly switches back and forth between transmitting and receiving. The code QSK communicates that an operator can hear another station's signal and that the detected station can break in on the user's transmission.

Subelement G2 – Operating Procedures

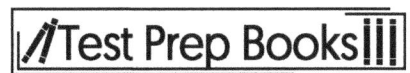

Q-Signal	Reference	Question
QRG	Checking an operator's exact frequency	What is your exact frequency?
QRL*	Testing if a frequency is busy	I am busy. Are you busy?
QRM	Transmission interference	Does my transmission have interference? (1-5)
QRN*	Static problems	Are you having trouble with static? (1-5)
QRO	Increase power	Should I increase power?
QRP	Decrease power	Should I decrease power?
QRQ	Send faster	Should I send faster?
QRS*	Send slower	Should I send more slowly?
QRT	Stop sending	Should I stop sending?
QRU	Having a message	Do you have a message for me?
QRV	Readiness	Are you ready?
QRX	Scheduling next call	When will you call again?
QRZ	Identifying caller	Who is calling me?
QSB	Fading signals	Are my signals fading?
QSK	Breaking in	May I break in on this transmission?
QSL*	Acknowledging receipt, 10-4, Roger	Could you acknowledge receipt?
QSO	Direct communication	Can you transmit directly?
QSP	Relaying	Will you relay to ___?
QST	General address	Denotes a message for all hams
QSX	Listening	Will you listen to _____ on _____ kHz?
QSY	Changing frequencies	Should I change to another frequency?
QTC	Number of messages	How many messages will you send?
QTH	Location	What is your location?
QTR	Time	What time is it?

43

G2D

Volunteer Monitoring Program

To ensure ham users follow federal communication regulations and encourage good amateur practice, the ARRL has an agreement with the FCC establishing the Volunteer Monitor program. **The Volunteer Monitor program** is an organization of volunteer operators trained to monitor radio frequencies for violations and remedy misconduct. This means amateur radio regulates itself through volunteer policing of ham-allocated airwaves.

When a member of the Volunteer Monitor program discovers Part 97 violations, they report to and work with the program administrator to notify the offender and rectify the issue. Often, volunteer monitors mail rule-breakers postcards reiterating FCC regulations; they also send positive reinforcement to operators with outstanding conduct. In extreme cases, the program handles violations by referring them to the FCC for disciplinary action.

Volunteer monitors, sometimes called **official observers (OO)**, must locate stations breaking FCC regulations. Fox hunting, an activity that operators often use to develop tracking skills during recreational radio sporting, is the main way to find another station's signal. Amateur radio sport offers many popular contests every weekend that provide ham operators a chance to develop new skills and compete for awards. In radio sport, **fox hunting** refers to **hidden transmitter hunts** in which amateurs employ directional antennas to triangulate on a transmission.

When fox hunting is used by OOs, the volunteer monitors act as "hounds," seeking offending signals known as "foxes." Hidden transmitter hunts play an integral role in identifying stations operating outside of the FCC regulatory framework or amateur frequency allocations. In any scenario, whether radio sport or volunteer monitoring, operators must follow FCC regulations.

HF Operations

CW operates on HF bands. To begin transmitting using Morse code, operators should set their mode to CW and tune their station to a frequency in the bottom section of a HF band. Amateurs may encounter static during transmission due to ionospheric conditions that disproportionately affect lower HF frequencies, especially during the summertime. Operators may opt to transmit with a lower power output when experiencing such conditions.

An **azimuthal projection map** is a tool that helps amateur radio operators locate stations and determine directions and distances between them. Directions on azimuthal projections are based on **true bearings**, meaning the location's position relative to true north, or geodetic north, in degrees. To interpret an azimuthal projection map, amateurs should read the map as though they are in the center and the map radiates out directionally from that point. When contacting another station, operators must decide between sending the signal via the short- or long-path. If they select the long-path, they should direct the antenna 180 degrees from the beginning of the short-path, thereby pointing it in the opposite direction.

Subelement G2 – Operating Procedures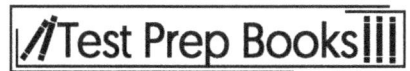

Operators should call CQ to locate a conversation partner. Protocol for making contact requires hams to repeat "CQ" several times before stating their call sign using the standard NATO phonetic alphabet several times. Then, hams should listen for a response. It may take several tries to find a good contact. For example, a control operator looking for a receiving station would call "CQ. CQ. CQ. This is November Five Alpha Bravo Charlie. November Five Alpha Bravo Charlie, standing by for a call." Many operators maintain a **station log** to track contacts, awards, and other crucial information. The FCC does not require this kind of station record, but it can prove beneficial in case the FCC reaches out with an inquiry.

G2E

Digital Mode Operating Procedures

As discussed in earlier sections, **radioteletype (RTTY)** refers to a digital mode of radio telecommunications in which operators send messages by encoding letters using dual modulating tones, which, usually, hams space 170 Hz apart from one another. The transceiver at the receiving station then decodes the two tones to deliver messages. In contrast to voice modes, RTTY always transmits on LSB. Additionally, there are different ways to modulate transmitted tones.

Frequency shift keying (FSK) is one of the most common types of digital modulation used to generate coded tones, and there are several variations on this method. **Binary frequency shift keying (BFSK)**, the most used method of FSK, transmits binary coded messages by modulating between SSB carrier signal frequencies. On RTTY, the shift between modulated frequencies usually has 170 MHz distance. BFSK employs mark and space frequencies to transmit **binary code (1s and 0s)**; 1s are **mark frequencies** and 0s are **space frequencies**.

Audio frequency shift keying (AFSK) refers to a subtype of FSK. In AFSK, stations transmit digital information by shifting back and forth between two pitches of an audio frequency, using audio oscillators, to generate a coded binary signal. ASFK and FSK both generate the same type of modulation. However, ASFK differs from FSK in that they utilize different basebands to modulate the audio signal; AFSK modulates the **audio baseband signal** while FSK uses a **polar binary baseband signal**.

The receiving station must then demodulate the signal, often using the Goertzel Algorithm, to decode the message. The **Goertzel Algorithm** is an iterative method of processing digital signals that demodulates transmissions by applying a mathematical digital filter operation to an input sequence derived from discrete frequencies. Difficulties decoding an RTTY signal usually indicates an operator error. The operator may have selected the incorrect baud rate, set the station to the incorrect sideband, or programmed the decoding function to reverse the order of mark and space frequencies.

There are other types of digital communication methods used in amateur radio. Alternative digital operating modes solve common issues encountered under subpar conditions for RTTY operations. For example, **WSJT** is an open-source computer program that facilitates amateur communication on weak RF signals by diversifying available digital signal processing methods. Operators can use this program to apply AFSK to modes like JT65, JT9, and FT8 and transmit digital messages over weak signals. These non-RTTY transmissions almost always transmit on HF using the USB.

Subelement G2 – Operating Procedures

JT65 and JT9 are two operating modes named for amateur operator Joe Taylor, who discovered binary pulsars. **JT65** is used for weak, slowly varying signals, such as those found in **Earth-Moon-Earth (EME)** paths, also known as **moonbounce paths**. This mode can decode transmissions below the noise floor, so it enables amateurs to decode signals that may not be audible to humans. Encoded JT65 messages are transmitted via 65-tone MFSK. **JT9** is usually used for MF and HF bands. It decodes and encodes in the same way as JT65. However, it modulates using 9-FSK, which takes up significantly less bandwidth than JT65 digital signal processing.

FT8, or Franke-Taylor design, is a faster processing technique that uses 8-FSK. It completes contacts up to four times faster than slower digital processing modes like JT65 and JT9. FT8 can decode multiple signals in the passband by tracking how signal spectrum data changes over time with visualization software that shows intervallic spectral density. FT8 was not designed for lengthy conversations, so operators generally use this mode to transmit simple information like call signs, signal reports, and azimuthal grid locations. For the decoding function to work, FT8 mode requires exact timing; therefore, operators using this mode should ensure their station computer clock runs within one second of accuracy.

Packet Teleprinting on Radio (PACTOR) combines aspects of PACKET and AMTOR ARQ digital modulation to facilitate digital communication over weak or staticky signals on HF bands. It is a semi-automated mode. Like RTTY and many digital modes, it uses FSK to transmit messages, but PACTOR also employs **automated repeat query (ARQ)** technology to correct errors in real-time. Generally, amateur operators transmit with PACTOR on frequencies between 1 MHz and 30MHz. PACTOR only works for communications between two stations, so it's impossible to introduce a third station (i.e., join a contact) into conversations conducted using this protocol.

A **modem** is a device that modulates digital signals to send messages over RF and demodulates received signals; in other words, modems code and decode RF transmissions. **Modulating** means conveying information by changing waveform shapes. There are two main types of modulation used in amateur radio – **Amplitude Modulation (AM)** and **Frequency Modulation (FM)**. Operators can switch their modem to communication monitoring mode to check if another PACTOR user is transmitting on a particular channel, indicating a busy signal. Monitoring listens for a signal on a certain frequency without attempting contact.

WINMOR is a now-deprecated digital program that ran off PACTOR to send emails over radio frequencies. It was replaced by **Amateur Radio Digital Open Protocol (ARDOP)** and **VARA HF**. These newer protocols work similarly to WINMOR but can transmit much faster. While WINMOR could only transmit at 1,000 bps, ARDOP sends at up to 4,000 bps, and VARA HF transmits at up to 7,000 bps. Like most radio transmissions, these modes are susceptible to interference. To diagnose RFI while using PACTOR-based digital modes, operators should notice slow transmissions with long pauses, recurring timeouts or reloads, and difficulty or inability to make contact.

Winlink, formerly **Radio Mail Server (RMS) Express**, is a global messaging service that operates via amateur and governmental radio frequencies. It is the standard international network utilized for ham radio email. Often, Winlink is used in emergency communications and relief since it can facilitate communication when users lack internet access. Winlink can also integrate radio frequencies with any available Internet to strengthen transmission of email messages. It used to run using a global network of independent servers; however, since 2017, the program has operated using **Amazon Web Services (AWS)** servers. Winlink works by transmitting packet messages over HF SSB transmitters and receivers

Subelement G2 – Operating Procedures

that are tied to a modem like PACTOR, ARDOP, VARA HF, or Automatic Link Establishment (ALE). Winlink users must have the appropriate ham license for the chosen frequency.

Phase Shift Key, 31 Baud (PSK31), one of the simplest digital modes, is a type of noise-resistant phase shift keying that facilitates communication between keyboards. To run PSK31 software, operators must have an SSB transceiver, an antenna, and a computer with a soundcard. The data rate for PSK31 is 31.25 bauds. PSK31 transmits on a frequency right below that of RTTY, close to 14.070 MHz. Modulation can be either **binary** without error correction or **quadrature** with error correction. Amateur operators encode messages with a **Varicode character schematic** which generates the ASCII ten-bit set. Automatic leveling controls set to 0 reduces the possibility of signal splatter (distortion).

A **waterfall display** helps operators visualize PSK31 transmissions by showing frequency (horizontal), time (vertical), and signal strength intensity on a continuous, dynamic, colored data visualization. Overmodulation is indicated when the waterfall display shows one or multiple vertical lines next to a PSK31 signal.

A **DE-9**, often incorrectly referred to as a DB-9, is a type of D-subminiature coaxial connector used to connect serial data ports. It has a 5-4 pin and socket layout. A DE-9 must have at least four conductors, two that transmit and two that receive. USB connectors have largely replaced serial ports, but a lot of radio equipment, especially older hardware, relies on the standard DE-9 connector. Operators can purchase a **USB-to-serial adaptor** to connect modern computer ports to traditional hardware that relies on the DE-9.

Digital gateways facilitate connections between operators. To contact a digital messaging system gateway station, amateurs should tune transmissions to the station's particular frequency. There are some bands and frequencies used more often for digital modes. For example, the 20m band, specifically between 14.070 and 14.112 MHz, is commonly used for digital transmissions. On the 80m band, operators transmit on digital modes between 3570 and 3600 kHz to make contact. Generally, amateur radio transmissions use CW to transmit over the lower frequencies in each band, SSB for the upper frequencies, and digital modes in the center of the band.

Subelement G2 – Questions

G2A

1. Which mode is most commonly used for voice communications on frequencies of 14 MHz or higher?
    a. Upper sideband
    b. Lower sideband
    c. Suppressed sideband
    d. Double sideband

2. Which mode is most commonly used for voice communications on the 160-, 75-, and 40-meter bands?
    a. Upper sideband
    b. Lower sideband
    c. Suppressed sideband
    d. Double sideband

3. Which mode is most commonly used for SSB voice communications in the VHF and UHF bands?
    a. Upper sideband
    b. Lower sideband
    c. Suppressed sideband
    d. Double sideband

4. Which mode is most commonly used for voice communications on the 17- and 12-meter bands?
    a. Upper sideband
    b. Lower sideband
    c. Suppressed sideband
    d. Double sideband

5. Which mode of voice communication is most commonly used on the HF amateur bands?
    a. Frequency modulation
    b. Double sideband
    c. Single sideband
    d. Single phase modulation

6. Which of the following is an advantage of using single sideband, as compared to other analog voice modes on the HF amateur bands?
    a. Very high-fidelity voice modulation
    b. Less subject to interference from atmospheric static crashes
    c. Ease of tuning on receive and immunity to impulse noise
    d. Less bandwidth used and greater power efficiency

7. Which of the following statements is true of single sideband (SSB)?
    a. Only one sideband and the carrier are transmitted; the other sideband is suppressed
    b. Only one sideband is transmitted; the other sideband and carrier are suppressed
    c. SSB is the only voice mode authorized on the 20-, 15-, and 10-meter amateur bands
    d. SSB is the only voice mode authorized on the 160-, 75-, and 40-meter amateur bands

8. What is the recommended way to break into a phone contact?
   a. Say "QRZ" several times, followed by your call sign
   b. Say your call sign once
   c. Say "Breaker Breaker"
   d. Say "CQ" followed by the call sign of either station

9. Why do most amateur stations use lower sideband on the 160-, 75-, and 40-meter bands?
   a. Lower sideband is more efficient than upper sideband at these frequencies
   b. Lower sideband is the only sideband legal on these frequency bands
   c. Because it is fully compatible with an AM detector
   d. It is commonly accepted amateur practice

10. Which of the following statements is true of VOX operation versus PTT operation?
    a. The received signal is more natural sounding
    b. It allows "hands free" operation
    c. It occupies less bandwidth
    d. It provides more power output

11. Generally, who should respond to a station in the contiguous 48 states calling "CQ DX"?
    a. Any caller is welcome to respond
    b. Only stations in Germany
    c. Any stations outside the lower 48 states
    d. Only contest stations

12. What control is typically adjusted for proper ALC setting on a single sideband transceiver?
    a. RF clipping level
    b. Transmit audio or microphone gain
    c. Antenna inductance or capacitance
    d. Attenuator level

G2B

1. Which of the following is true concerning access to frequencies?
   a. Nets have priority
   b. QSOs in progress have priority
   c. Except during emergencies, no amateur station has priority access to any frequency
   d. Contest operations should yield to non-contest use of frequencies

2. What is the first thing you should do if you are communicating with another amateur station and hear a station in distress break in?
   a. Inform your local emergency coordinator
   b. Acknowledge the station in distress and determine what assistance may be needed
   c. Immediately decrease power to avoid interfering with the station in distress
   d. Immediately cease all transmissions

3. What is good amateur practice if propagation changes during a contact creating interference from other stations using the frequency?
   a. Advise the interfering stations that you are on the frequency and that you have priority
   b. Decrease power and continue to transmit
   c. Attempt to resolve the interference problem with the other stations in a mutually acceptable manner
   d. Switch to the opposite sideband

4. When selecting a CW transmitting frequency, what minimum separation from other stations should be used to minimize interference to stations on adjacent frequencies?
   a. 5 Hz to 50 Hz
   b. 150 Hz to 500 Hz
   c. 1 kHz to 3 kHz
   d. 3 kHz to 6 kHz

5. When selecting an SSB transmitting frequency, what minimum separation should be used to minimize interference to stations on adjacent frequencies?
   a. 5 Hz to 50 Hz
   b. 150 Hz to 500 Hz
   c. 2 kHz to 3 kHz
   d. Approximately 6 kHz

6. How can you avoid harmful interference on an apparently clear frequency before calling CQ on CW or phone?
   a. Send "QRL?" on CW, followed by your call sign; or, if using phone, ask if the frequency is in use, followed by your call sign
   b. Listen for 2 minutes before calling CQ
   c. Send the letter "V" in Morse code several times and listen for a response, or say "test" several times and listen for a response
   d. Send "QSY" on CW or if using phone, announce "the frequency is in use," then give your call sign and listen for a response

7. Which of the following complies with commonly accepted amateur practice when choosing a frequency on which to initiate a call?
   a. Listen on the frequency for at least two minutes to be sure it is clear
   b. Identify your station by transmitting your call sign at least 3 times
   c. Follow the voluntary band plan
   d. All these choices are correct

8. What is the voluntary band plan restriction for US stations transmitting within the 48 contiguous states in the 50.1 MHz to 50.125 MHz band segment?
   a. Only contacts with stations not within the 48 contiguous states
   b. Only contacts with other stations within the 48 contiguous states
   c. Only digital contacts
   d. Only SSTV contacts

9. Who may be the control operator of an amateur station transmitting in RACES to assist relief operations during a disaster?
    a. Only a person holding an FCC-issued amateur operator license
    b. Only a RACES net control operator
    c. A person holding an FCC-issued amateur operator license or an appropriate government official
    d. Any control operator when normal communication systems are operational

10. Which of the following is good amateur practice for net management?
    a. Always use multiple sets of phonetics during check-in
    b. Have a backup frequency in case of interference or poor conditions
    c. Transmit the full net roster at the beginning of every session
    d. All these choices are correct

11. How often may RACES training drills and tests be routinely conducted without special authorization?
    a. No more than 1 hour per month
    b. No more than 2 hours per month
    c. No more than 1 hour per week
    d. No more than 2 hours per week

G2C

1. Which of the following describes full break-in CW operation (QSK)?
    a. Breaking stations send the Morse code prosign "BK"
    b. Automatic keyers, instead of hand keys, are used to send Morse code
    c. An operator must activate a manual send/receive switch before and after every transmission
    d. Transmitting stations can receive between code characters and elements

2. What should you do if a CW station sends "QRS?"
    a. Send slower
    b. Change frequency
    c. Increase your power
    d. Repeat everything twice

3. What does it mean when a CW operator sends "KN" at the end of a transmission?
    a. No US stations should call
    b. Operating full break-in
    c. Listening only for a specific station or stations
    d. Closing station now

4. What does the Q signal "QRL?" mean?
    a. "Will you keep the frequency clear?"
    b. "Are you operating full break-in?" or "Can you operate full break-in?"
    c. "Are you listening only for a specific station?"
    d. "Are you busy?" or "Is this frequency in use?"

5. What is the best speed to use when answering a CQ in Morse code?
   a. The fastest speed at which you are comfortable copying, but no slower than the CQ
   b. The fastest speed at which you are comfortable copying, but no faster than the CQ
   c. At the standard calling speed of 10 wpm
   d. At the standard calling speed of 5 wpm

6. What does the term "zero beat" mean in CW operation?
   a. Matching the speed of the transmitting station
   b. Operating split to avoid interference on frequency
   c. Sending without error
   d. Matching the transmit frequency to the frequency of a received signal

7. When sending CW, what does a "C" mean when added to the RST report?
   a. Chirpy or unstable signal
   b. Report was read from an S meter rather than estimated
   c. 100 percent copy
   d. Key clicks

8. What prosign is sent to indicate the end of a formal message when using CW?
   a. SK
   b. BK
   c. AR
   d. KN

9. What does the Q signal "QSL" mean?
   a. Send slower
   b. We have already confirmed the contact
   c. I have received and understood
   d. We have worked before

10. What does the Q signal "QRN" mean?
    a. Send more slowly
    b. Stop sending
    c. Zero beat my signal
    d. I am troubled by static

11. What does the Q signal "QRV" mean?
    a. You are sending too fast
    b. There is interference on the frequency
    c. I am quitting for the day
    d. I am ready to receive

G2D

1. What is the Volunteer Monitor Program?
   a. Amateur volunteers who are formally enlisted to monitor the airwaves for rules violations
   b. Amateur volunteers who conduct amateur licensing examinations
   c. Amateur volunteers who conduct frequency coordination for amateur VHF repeaters
   d. Amateur volunteers who use their station equipment to help civil defense organizations in times of emergency

2. Which of the following are objectives of the Volunteer Monitor Program?
   a. To conduct efficient and orderly amateur licensing examinations
   b. To provide emergency and public safety communications
   c. To coordinate repeaters for efficient and orderly spectrum usage
   d. To encourage amateur radio operators to self-regulate and comply with the rules

3. What procedure may be used by Volunteer Monitors to localize a station whose continuous carrier is holding a repeater on in their area?
   a. Compare vertical and horizontal signal strengths on the input frequency
   b. Compare beam headings on the repeater input from their home locations with that of other Volunteer Monitors
   c. Compare signal strengths between the input and output of the repeater
   d. All these choices are correct

4. Which of the following describes an azimuthal projection map?
   a. A map that shows accurate land masses
   b. A map that shows true bearings and distances from a specific location
   c. A map that shows the angle at which an amateur satellite crosses the equator
   d. A map that shows the number of degrees longitude that an amateur satellite appears to move westward at the equator with each orbit

5. Which of the following indicates that you are looking for an HF contact with any station?
   a. Sign your call sign once, followed by the words "listening for a call" -- if no answer, change frequency and repeat
   b. Say "QTC" followed by "this is" and your call sign -- if no answer, change frequency and repeat
   c. Repeat "CQ" a few times, followed by "this is," then your call sign a few times, then pause to listen, repeat as necessary
   d. Transmit an unmodulated carried for approximately 10 seconds, followed by "this is" and your call sign, and pause to listen -- repeat as necessary

6. How is a directional antenna pointed when making a "long-path" contact with another station?
   a. Toward the rising sun
   b. Along the gray line
   c. 180 degrees from the station's short path heading
   d. Toward the north

7. Which of the following are examples of the NATO Phonetic Alphabet?
   a. Able, Baker, Charlie, Dog
   b. Adam, Boy, Charles, David
   c. America, Boston, Canada, Denmark
   d. Alpha, Bravo, Charlie, Delta

8. Why do many amateurs keep a station log?
   a. The FCC requires a log of all international contacts
   b. The FCC requires a log of all international third-party traffic
   c. The log provides evidence of operation needed to renew a license without retest
   d. To help with a reply if the FCC requests information about your station

9. Which of the following is required when participating in a contest on HF frequencies?
   a. Submit a log to the contest sponsor
   b. Send a QSL card to the stations worked, or QSL via Logbook of The World
   c. Identify your station according to normal FCC regulations
   d. All these choices are correct

10. What is QRP operation?
    a. Remote piloted model control
    b. Low-power transmit operation
    c. Transmission using Quick Response Protocol
    d. Traffic relay procedure net operation

11. Why are signal reports typically exchanged at the beginning of an HF contact?
    a. To allow each station to operate according to conditions
    b. To be sure the contact will count for award programs
    c. To follow standard radiogram structure
    d. To allow each station to calibrate their frequency display

G2E

1. Which mode is normally used when sending RTTY signals via AFSK with an SSB transmitter?
   a. USB
   b. DSB
   c. CW
   d. LSB

2. What is VARA?
   a. A low signal-to-noise digital mode used for EME (moonbounce)
   b. A digital protocol used with Winlink
   c. A radio direction finding system used on VHF and UHF
   d. A DX spotting system using a network of software defined radios

3. What symptoms may result from other signals interfering with a PACTOR or VARA transmission?
   a. Frequent retries or timeouts
   b. Long pauses in message transmission
   c. Failure to establish a connection between stations
   d. All these choices are correct

4. Which of the following is good practice when choosing a transmitting frequency to answer a station calling CQ using FT8?
    a. Always call on the station's frequency
    b. Call on any frequency in the waterfall except the station's frequency
    c. Find a clear frequency during the same time slot as the calling station
    d. Find a clear frequency during the alternate time slot to the calling station

5. What is the standard sideband for JT65, JT9, FT4, or FT8 digital signal when using AFSK?
    a. LSB
    b. USB
    c. DSB
    d. SSB

6. What is the most common frequency shift for RTTY emissions in the amateur HF bands?
    a. 85 Hz
    b. 170 Hz
    c. 425 Hz
    d. 850 Hz

7. Which of the following is required when using FT8?
    a. A special hardware modem
    b. Computer time accurate to within approximately 1 second
    c. Receiver attenuator set to -12 dB
    d. A vertically polarized antenna

8. In what segment of the 20-meter band are most digital mode operations commonly found?
    a. At the bottom of the slow-scan TV segment, near 14.230 MHz
    b. At the top of the SSB phone segment, near 14.325 MHz
    c. In the middle of the CW segment, near 14.100 MHz
    d. Between 14.070 MHz and 14.100 MHz

9. How do you join a contact between two stations using the PACTOR protocol?
    a. Send broadcast packets containing your call sign while in MONITOR mode
    b. Transmit a steady carrier until the PACTOR protocol times out and disconnects
    c. Joining an existing contact is not possible, PACTOR connections are limited to two stations
    d. Send a NAK code

10. Which of the following is a way to establish contact with a digital messaging system gateway station?
    a. Send an email to the system control operator
    b. Send QRL in Morse code
    c. Respond when the station broadcasts its SSID
    d. Transmit a connect message on the station's published frequency

11. What is the primary purpose of an Amateur Radio Emergency Data Network (AREDN) mesh network?
    a. To provide FM repeater coverage in remote areas
    b. To provide real time propagation data by monitoring amateur radio transmissions worldwide
    c. To provide high-speed data services during an emergency or community event
    d. To provide DX spotting reports to aid contesters and DXers

12. Which of the following describes Winlink?
    a. An amateur radio wireless network to send and receive email on the internet
    b. A form of Packet Radio
    c. A wireless network capable of both VHF and HF band operation
    d. All of the above

13. What is another name for a Winlink Remote Message Server?
    a. Terminal Node Controller
    b. Gateway
    c. RJ-45
    d. Printer/Server

14. What could be wrong if you cannot decode an RTTY or other FSK signal even though it is apparently tuned in properly?
    a. The mark and space frequencies may be reversed
    b. You may have selected the wrong baud rate
    c. You may be listening on the wrong sideband
    d. All these choices are correct

15. Which of the following is a common location for FT8?
    a. Anywhere in the voice portion of the band
    b. Anywhere in the CW portion of the band
    c. Approximately 14.074 MHz to 14.077 MHz
    d. Approximately 14.110 MHz to 14.113 MHz

Subelement G2 – Answer Key

G2A

1. A	7. B
2. B	8. B
3. A	9. D
4. A	10. B
5. C	11. C
6. D	12. B

G2B

1. C	7. C
2. B	8. A
3. C	9. A
4. B	10. B
5. C	11. C
6. A	

G2C

1. D	7. A
2. A	8. C
3. C	9. C
4. D	10. D
5. B	11. D
6. D	

G2D

1. A	7. D
2. D	8. D
3. B	9. C
4. B	10. B
5. C	11. A
6. C	

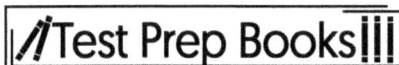

G2E

1. D	9. C
2. B	10. D
3. D	11. C
4. D	12. D
5. B	13. B
6. B	14. D
7. B	15. C
8. D	

Subelement G3 – Radio Wave Propagation

G3A

Sunspots and Solar Radiation

Propagation is how radio waves travel; "how" refers to the characteristics defining a signal's direction, distribution, and mode of transmission. HF transmissions travel via skywaves, which means antennas bounce HF signals off the Earth's ionosphere, or upper atmosphere, at an angle to refract them toward a receiving station. The **ionosphere** is the ionized gaseous particulate layer of Earth's atmosphere embedded in the mesosphere and thermosphere. Signals transmitted in this manner are called **skywaves**.

The sun's rays charge particles in the ionosphere, creating a gaseous layer of ions (energized particles) mixed with neutral atoms and molecules. Solar radiation heat molecules in the ionosphere, causing them to lose electrons and ionizing some of the particles. The ionosphere absorbs all solar radiation with a wavelength smaller than 200 nanometers and releases it back into space as carbon dioxide (CO_2) and nitric oxide (NO). Skywave propagation works because the charged gases that make up the ionosphere give it a conductive property. This conductivity facilitates **skywave refraction**, bending radio signals back to the Earth when they reach the upper atmosphere.

Solar radiation increases ionization levels in the ionosphere's molecular composition, and greater ionization levels have better radio propagation. Therefore, HF propagation is influenced by solar activity and its impact on ionospheric conditions. HF bands require high solar activity to charge the ionosphere sufficiently for successful propagation.

When conditions are good, operators can make longer distance contacts with more band possibilities and lower power outputs. Other times, conditions inhibit communication. For example, HF skywave transmissions with shorter wavelengths, such as 15m, 12m, and 10m, have a lower likelihood of success when it comes to **distance (DX)** contacts. Communication on these bands may not be possible during times of reduced solar activity. However, the volatility of ionospheric conditions makes communicating on shortwave bands even more exciting during periods of high solar activity.

Solar radiation includes the sun's emissions which span the electromagnetic spectrum, including UV radiation and X-rays. This radiation generates solar winds, which are composed of ionized radiation, plasma, and particles that stream constantly from the sun's surface and atmosphere. Solar flares are eruptions on the sun's surface, usually near sunspots that have increased plasma and particle emissions. In some cases, solar flares can lead to coronal mass ejection (CMEs).

Sunspots are areas that are comparatively cooler on the sun's surface, so they appear darker than surrounding parts. They emerge because of the interaction between surface plasma and sun's magnetic field and can manifest as a single sunspot or clustered group. The number of sunspots increases and decreases as the solar cycle progresses. They are one of the only solar indicators visible to the human eye, so operators can use them to determine solar activity. Sunspots heighten the probability of successful HF propagations, so amateurs should look for higher sunspot numbers when selecting communications.

Subelement G3 – Radio Wave Propagation

Solar emissions are **cyclical**. The **solar cycle** progresses over an **11-year span**, meaning that different years produce different levels of radiation. During the solar cycle, the sun waxes and wanes in intensity, and emissions vary greatly depending on the solar phase. Sunspot activity generally peaks every 11 years. There is also a **28-day cycle** that coincides with the sun's rotation; in other words, it takes 28 days for the sun to complete one rotation around its axis. Solar data is smoothed, or averaged, to make the sporadic nature of short-term changes in sunspots easier to analyze and predict.

The defining features of the solar cycle emerge and disappear on overlapping timelines, so the 11-year period represents an inexact frame of reference for the solar cycle based on average historical estimations. During **solar maximum**, lots of sunspots, solar flares, and solar emissions appear. Hundreds of sunspots may be visible during a solar cycle's peak. Generally, scientists detect more auroras and volatile ionospheric conditions. During **solar minimum**, there are fewer sunspots and solar flares, and there may be days or weeks when no solar activity is detected.

Ionospheric Disturbances

Earth's magnetic field is called the **magnetosphere**. It protects the Earth from solar winds – the sun's continuously charged particle emissions. Any charged emissions directed toward Earth will influence the density and composition of the ionosphere as well as interact with the magnetosphere; therefore, all ionized particles will change HF radio propagation conditions and possibilities.

The magnetosphere is generated by the Earth's liquid outer core, – composed of fluid nickel and iron – which churns in whirlpools agitated by the rotation of the planet, generating strong, fluctuating electric currents. These rotating electric currents create a magnetic field around the Earth via the **dynamo effect** as the planet turns and the iron core slowly cools and solidifies. For this reason, the magnetosphere is also referred to as the **geomagnetic field**.

The magnetic field forms the basis for directional navigation with magnetic compasses and shields Earth from atmospheric erosion by solar winds, solar flares, and coronal mass ejections. The magnetic poles differ from the geodetic poles. Additionally, the magnetosphere's strength fluctuates, and its poles drift gradually, reversing positions roughly every 300,000 years.

Disturbances in the magnetosphere, as well as ionizing solar emissions, can precipitate ionospheric storms that cause disruptions in magnetic instruments and produce RF interference on high and very high frequency bands. Geomagnetic storms make signals noisier and complicate or eliminate radio propagation possibilities. Three types of unpredictable disturbances negatively affect propagation typically: solar flares, coronal holes, and sudden disappearing filaments (SDFs).

Solar flares, intense eruptions of radiated energy particulate spewed from the sun's surface, most often occur during the peak of the solar cycle. When solar flares occur, X-ray emissions can cause a **Sudden Ionospheric Disturbance (SID)** and heighten RF absorption in the D-layer. An SID can disrupt daytime radio communication on high frequency bands from 2 to 30-MHz; usually, signals transmitted over lower frequencies experience more difficulties than those on higher frequencies within the HF portion of the electromagnetic spectrum. The particles emitted in a solar flare enter the Earth's atmosphere as plasma, or ionized gas. Due to its highly energized molecular composition, plasma can cause major disruptions in RF transmissions when it meets the Earth's magnetosphere. **Polar Cap Absorption (PCA)** can also occur because of solar flares.

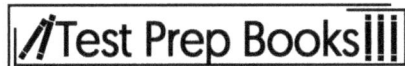

Subelement G3 – Radio Wave Propagation

A **coronal hole** is an anomalous dark hole in the sun's outer atmospheric layer, known as the **corona**; they are not visible to the human eye. While scientists haven't reached a consensus on the origin of coronal holes, some posit that they derive from residual matter left by older sunspots, somewhat like a fossil or skeleton.

A coronal hole is a part of the sun with a comparatively lower temperature than the rest of its surface. Typically, coronal holes happen as the solar cycle declines. Coronal holes can manifest as singular or recurring solar events; when they persist, appearing on certain days each month over a longer period, scientists refer to the phenomenon as a recurring coronal hole. Coronal holes emit solar wind at double the average speed, so they can increase HF radio disturbances.

A **Sudden Disappearing Filament (SDF)** is another type of ionospheric disturbance caused by solar activity. **Solar filaments** are prominent loops of plasma formed by the sun's magnetic field. When the heliosphere is destabilized, it can cause one of these filaments to suddenly eject and arc away from the sun's surface towards Earth.

Solar winds are streams of charged particles moving at 40 km per second. When solar winds meet an area where the Earth's magnetic field overlaps with the ionosphere, the energetic confluence creates an aurora. Since plasma emitted as solar wind travels at the speed of light, energized solar particles reach Earth approximately 8 minutes after departing from the sun's magnetic field. This means that radio propagation experiences ionospheric disturbances from solar radiation, including UV emissions and X-rays, within 8 minutes once a solar flare occurs.

A **radiation storm** occurs when energetic solar protons collide with the upper atmosphere close to the north and south poles, enhancing the D layer's absorption capabilities. Radiation storms are often caused by solar flares, which enhance the D layer when x-ray photons ionize the atoms and molecules in the ionosphere's bottom layer. The extreme ionization of the D layer can lead to a radio blackout in severe cases.

Coronal Mass Ejections (CMEs) are sudden bursts of energy ejected from sunspots that can cause sever geomatic storms. Because they increase solar wind speed, they have a strong, destabilizing impact on the Earth's magnetosphere. Generally, it takes CME particles about 20 to 40 hours to affect radio signals because they do not travel as quickly as UV and X-ray radiation from solar flares. Therefore, scientists can analyze X-rays to predict aspects of incoming CME impacts on radio propagation.

Geomagnetic storms are disruptions in the earth's magnetosphere that can temporarily inhibit or eliminate HF propagation at high latitudes. High latitudes, such as those found near the Earth's north and south poles, experience more severe ionospheric disturbances than other places during geomagnetic storms since they attract **solar wind particles** (energized plasma molecules ejected from the heliosphere).

When solar radiation reaches Earth, the magnetic field deflects the charged particles, which themselves are magnetized, by attracting them to the planet's two magnetic poles. Without this protection, solar winds would destroy the ozone layer, allowing the sun's UV rays to reach the Earth unfiltered and warming the planet to an uninhabitable degree. Geomagnetic storms can lead to **radio blackouts** in severe cases

Solar particles travel along solar magnetic field lines radiating outward. As the sun rotates in its 28-day cycle, these emissions turn as well, which causes the plasma on the sun's surface to spiral and generate solar wind. Most solar wind is held in place by the sun's magnetic field, or **heliosphere**. When the portions of plasma spiraling into solar wind become heated to a sufficient degree, however, the heliosphere can no longer contain it. Solar wind then ejects away from the sun's surface in streams, some of which enter the ionosphere. Therefore, radio propagation changes cyclically based on the position of solar emissions as the sun turns over the course of these 28 days.

Auroras are colored lights emitted by ionized particles in the sky about 1000km above Earth's magnetic poles. This phenomenon occurs when geomagnetic compression induces magnetic reconnection. **Magnetic reconnection** is the phenomenon that causes charged solar particles to flow toward both ends of the Earth's geomagnetic poles. This process produces beautiful cosmic light shows, called auroras, in high-latitude locations known as **auroral zones**.

An **auroral oval** is a place where an aurora manifests at any given time. Earth has two major auroral phenomena: the northern lights and the southern lights. The lights viewed in the northern hemisphere are referred to as the **aurora borealis**, and those seen in the southern hemisphere are called the **aurora australis**. Sometimes, auroras can cause the same kinds of disturbances as solar flares or radiation storms – including geomagnetic storms.

While geomagnetic storms cause radio blackouts on HF bands, they can – surprisingly – generate a useful medium for DX ham communication through auroral propagation. **Auroral propagation** means leveraging ionospheric disturbances that produce auroras to facilitate improved VHF communication for distance transmissions. Auroras can serve as a transmission medium because they are extremely ionized and, therefore, able to reflect VHF signals much further – sometime more than 800 km away.

Geomagnetic Field and Stability Indices

Ionospheric conditions, and hence radio propagation, depend on how solar emissions interact with the Earth's magnetic field. Usually, a steady state of solar wind bombardment makes Earth's geomagnetic field relatively stable. Sometimes, however, extra emissions destabilize the magnetosphere. This destabilization creates geomagnetic storms. To anticipate these storms and report information that impacts radio communications, scientists must constantly monitor solar conditions and the Earth's magnetic field.

Because the ionosphere responds to the conditions of Earth's magnetosphere as well as space weather, amateur operators use two types of indices to predict radio propagation conditions: **solar indices** and **geomagnetic indices**. Several resources publish charts with both types of indices as well as other up-to-date solar-terrestrial data that helps hams determine HF and VHF conditions. Some websites publish solar imaging information, so hams can view current sunspots.

The **sunspot number (SN)**, also known as the **Wolf number**, measures the number of sunspot groups and individual sunspots. Scientists smooth out this measurement by taking daily averages to produce a monthly index they can use to track sunspots each month and generate a yearly average. The **smoothed sunspot number (SSN)** refers to a monthly SN, ranging from 0 to >200, used to produce the annual average. The SN helps predict future solar emissions as the solar cycle progresses. Higher SN values mean better propagation, since more sunspots radiate more ionizing emissions that charge the ionosphere.

The **Solar Flux Index (SFI)** measures solar flux, or the amount of noise in the atmosphere. The SFI is evaluated in **Solar Flux Units (SFUs)**, ranging from 60-300, which measure the strength of power

Subelement G3 – Radio Wave Propagation

received from solar emissions per unit area, per unit frequency. One SFU is equal to 10 watts per meter per Hz. SFUs change depending on the station location. The Penticton Radio Observatory in BC, Canada measures and records the SFI at 12:00pm daily by registering and analyzing noise levels generated by solar wind at 2800 MHz (10.7cm).

Solar flux is a useful metric because it is almost proportional to the level of ionizing radiation that reaches the Earth's upper atmosphere. A mathematical relationship exists between the sunspot number and solar flux. A simple calculation that closely approximates the true relationship between these variables is:

$$SFU = 73.4 + 0.62R$$

For HF propagation, higher values tend to work best (50 to 300 SFUs). At around 100 SFI, propagation is enhanced. Good DX usually starts around 150 SFUs; when operators encounter 150 SFUs for at least a few days in a row, they will probably have good DX communication. 300 SFUs represents excellent propagation conditions.

Hams use two main geomagnetic indices – the A Index and the K Index. These are station indices that analyze data taken with a magnetometer and report information about the magnetic field in specific locations. A **magnetometer** is an instrument used to measure geomagnetic activity by registering small changes in Earth's magnetosphere. There is a global magnetometer network that collectively monitors variations in the planet's magnetic field as conditions fluctuate.

The A Index and K Index are also used to produce planetary indices, referred to as Ap and Kp. To produce the Ap and Kp, station values are averaged to find generalized values for global geomagnetic conditions based on station indices.

The **K index** is a localized, quasi-logarithmic measurement taken every 3 hours globally. It monitors variations in magnetic flux for specific locations. Geophysicists use a magnetometer to measure variations in the Earth's magnetic field as compared to a baseline, meaning they compare the magnetometer readings to an average day with few ionospheric disturbances. A K index below 2 represents a relatively quiet and stable magnetosphere. They average the K Index measurements from 13 observatories worldwide to produce the **Planetary K Index** or **Kp**.

The **Kp** ranges from 0-9, and lower values indicate better propagation conditions. Since the K Index measures geomagnetic activity, operators usually want a stable number. Lower numbers mean fewer disruptions. The K Index cannot be averaged for the long-term because it is quasi-logarithmic; therefore, it is a short-term measurement. To get a long-term view of the magnetosphere's stability, scientists derive a second index from the K index, called the A index.

The **A Index** is a linear measurement that can be mathematically derived from the K index. Since the A Index is linear, scientists can use it to predict the magnetosphere's future activity in the long-term. A Index measurements are averaged to produce the **Planetary A index**, or **Ap**. The Ap ranges in value from 0- 400. Like the K Index, lower values represent better, more stable geomagnetic conditions. Ideally, hams should look for an A Index below 7 to guarantee successful propagation. The following chart shows the correlative relationship between the K Index and the A Index.

When looking at a graph or chart, operators should look for higher SFI, higher SN, and lower K and A index values. Relying on these factors can make it challenging to predict available shortwave frequency bands. However, operators can generally count on one portion of the HF spectrum regardless of ionospheric impacts caused by solar wind fluctuations – the 20m band. On 20 meters, hams can almost always propagate successfully during the day, and this makes it one of the most reliable and popular allocations used by amateur radio operators.

G3B

Maximum Usable Frequency

The **Maximum Usable Frequency (MUF)** is the highest frequency that can be used for skywave propagation to facilitate radio communication between two stations. Any frequency higher than the MUF will not refract because it will penetrate the ionosphere and continue traveling into space.

Several factors determine the MUF. For example, geographic factors, like the intended transmission distance and location, can change the highest frequency able to facilitate propagation. Additionally, temporal factors, such as date, season, and year, contribute to MUF determinations. Finally, ionospheric conditions, influenced by solar emissions as well as the Earth's geomagnetic stability, play a critical role.

In amateur radio, **attenuation** refers to the weakening of transmitted signals as they travel through a medium. For an HF transmission to experience the lowest amount of attenuation, or signal reduction, operators should use a frequency close to – but still below – the MUF.

Operators can identify the MUF for their location by tuning in to their desired HF band and listening for broadcasts from international beacons. If a control operator can hear an international beacon, then they can assume that frequency is within the usable frequency range. If the station transmits on a frequency that surpasses the MUF, the operator will not hear international beacons because the beacon signal is transmitting through the ionosphere out into space rather than refracting.

Lowest Usable Frequency

The **Lowest Usable Frequency (LUF)** refers to the lowest possible frequency an operator can use to communicate on HF bands. Generally, lower frequencies become more heavily attenuated upon reaching the D-layer because they cause more collisions between free electrons and neutral molecules, which makes it more difficult for the signal to pass through.

If an operator attempts to communicate on a frequency below the LUF threshold, the D-layer will absorb the frequency. Therefore, the signal will not refract off the ionosphere. The transmission essentially disappears. To avoid absorption during the day, the signal must be tuned to a higher frequency than the LUF. At night, the D layer disappears, and lower frequencies become available.

In between the LUF and MUF, propagation is possible because the frequency is high enough to avoid absorption but not so high that it passes through the ionosphere. In other words, the signal can "skip," meaning it can refract back to Earth and successfully transmit between stations globally. In some cases, ionospheric conditions occur such that the LUF is higher than the MUF. When this happens, HF transmissions are impossible since all HF signals will be absorbed.

Propagation

The ionosphere is the somewhat unpredictable, ionized, gaseous boundary between Earth and space. It is home to many satellites and astronomic equipment. For example, the **International Space Station (ISS)** is in the ionosphere. Charged particles can cause orbital drag on satellites. The ionosphere is extremely susceptible to external impacts. Both astronomic and terrestrial conditions affect the ionosphere.

Ionospheric conditions change based on the time of day. At night, ionized particles reconstitute into neutral particles since they are no longer being charged by the sun. Pressure waves caused by natural storm phenomena on Earth can change the ionosphere. It also reacts to magnetic and electric conditions in space - also known as space weather. The resulting temperature, density, and composition of the ionosphere influences the efficacy of radio propagation and sometimes can cause signal disruptions. Space weather can change or block an HF signal's transmission path, because the density of the ionosphere influences whether and how a radio wave is refracted.

Auroras, as discussed earlier, and airglow are the only parts of the ionosphere visible to the human eye. **Airglow** refers to light from the upper atmosphere created when atoms and molecules eject a photon, or light particle, to reduce their energy when they have become too energized by solar radiation. Different gases have different airglow colors. For example, UV airglow, red line airglow, and green line airglow are all commonly seen.

Each color depends on the type of gas being energized, its position within the ionosphere, and the way it has been charged. Scientists can study the location and behavior of gases in the ionosphere using these identifying colors. The **Ionospheric Connection Explorer (ICON)** uses airglow, invisible light wavelengths, and particle measurements to aggregate information that helps scientists study the ionosphere.

Global Scale Observations of the Limb and Disk (GOLD) refers to a tool for observing the ionosphere. Gold is a UV imaging spectrograph that takes images from its position in geostationary orbit, 22,000 miles above the surface of Brazil. The spectrograph splits light into wavelengths that generate images of invisible, far-UV light. The resulting photos are full-disk images (pictures of one side) of Earth's upper atmosphere. They reveal daily shifts in ionospheric conditions.

The **Appleton anomaly** refers to the equatorial ionization anomaly. In certain places, the Earth's magnetic field and the upper ionosphere converge. These areas of extreme ionization generate uprising plasma fountains at night, which gravity draws back towards Earth upon reaching a critical altitude. Consequently, the anomaly appears as two dense, arcing streams of light. They emerge from regions slightly north and south of the dip equator and diffuse along magnetospheric lines in either direction.

Line of sight propagation does not rely on refraction from ionosphere. In this type of propagation, the message moves directly from transmitter to receiver in a straight line. Line of sight is most useful for VHF communications. Sometimes line of sight propagation is not possible due to the Earth's curvature, obstructive terrain, or architectural blockages. In such cases, operators strategically employ antennas, satellites, and the Earth's ionosphere to refract signals to their destination.

In **groundwave propagation**, radio waves move from the transmitting antenna to the receiving antenna by moving across the Earth's surface. Groundwave propagation works best for short-range communication at lower frequencies since distance tapers as frequencies increase. Operators usually use vertically polarized antennas to transmit groundwaves, as in AM broadcast radio.

In **skywave propagation**, like in HF DX communications, radio waves travel from transmitter to receiver after being refracted off the ionosphere. Refraction means the ionosphere bends the RF signal, which determines where it comes back down to the Earth. Signals can even take multiple hops, bouncing back from the Earth back to the ionosphere and refracting back down. Signals can travel via a short or long path around the Earth. Long-path transmissions take longer to arrive at the receiving station. When any skywave signal reaches its destination, regardless of the path chosen, those on the receiving end will hear a delayed echo.

When beaming a signal from one station to another, there are essentially two paths the signal can take. For almost every situation imaginable, one of these paths will be shorter than the other; hence the two paths are often called the **short path** and **long path**. Neither path will quite be a straight line due to the curvature of the Earth and how the signal will be bounced off the ionosphere (more on that in a moment). The long path typically involves going the other way around the globe, and long-path propagation can sometimes result in a stronger signal compared to the short path. This is because the time of day can affect the strength of the ionosphere, particularly at night, so a long path may exploit or avoid a change in the ionosphere to make the signal more consistent.

Ionospheric refraction

Due to positively charged gas ions and free electrons that make up the ionosphere around the Earth, radio amateurs can employ a special trick called **ionospheric refraction** to bounce their signal farther across the globe. If HF signals are beamed at the right angle into the sky, the signals will bend back towards Earth because of the conductivity in the ionosphere. This allows a single radio signal to bounce back to the Earth at a greater distance, even bouncing back up into the ionosphere and refracting back to keep going. The following diagram shows this principle in action.

Action of Ionized Layer on HF Radio Wave Propagation

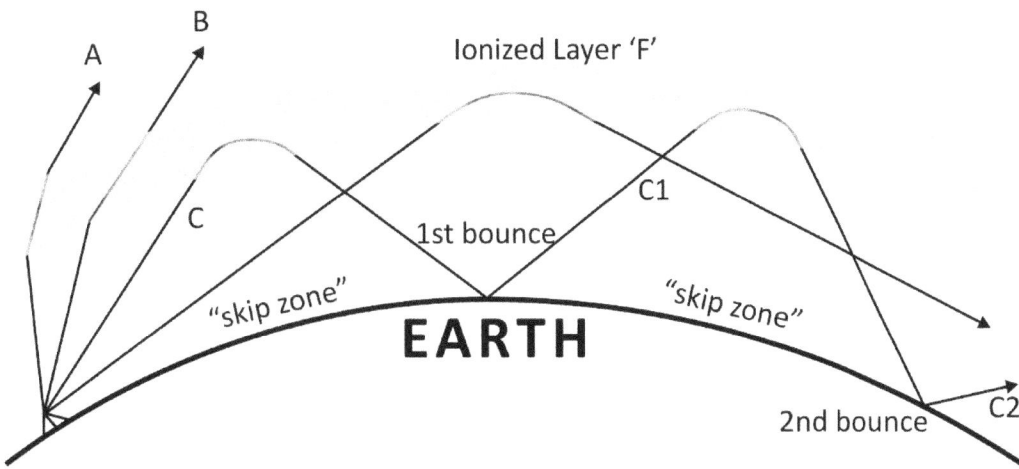

G3C

Ionospheric Regions

The **ionosphere** is a layer of Earth's upper atmosphere. Composed of densely packed molecules and electrically charged particles (ions), the ionosphere begins 60km above Earth and stretches up to 1000km. **Solar radiation** charges some of the suspended particles, and the resulting ionized gases are referred to as **plasma**. The ionosphere is made up of plasma and the remaining neutral atmosphere. In places where the ionosphere exists in the same place as magnetic fields, the air becomes beautifully lit. As discussed earlier, these areas are called **auroras**.

The ionosphere is made up of three parts of the mesosphere and thermosphere called the D, E, and F layers. Each layer plays a different role in amateur radio propagation. Ionospheric layers have different qualities during day and night. In the daytime, the **F layer** splits into two sections, called the **F1 (150km-220km)** and **F2 (220km-800km)** layers. The F2 layer bears the most responsibility for radio propagation since it is the uppermost layer and, therefore, refracts most radio transmission signals.

While the F layers typically refract most HF radio waves, the **E layer (90km-150km)** sometimes bends signals as well. However, generally signals pass through the E layer, and it does not have a major impact on skywave propagation. The **D layer (60km-90km)** absorbs low frequency RF. At night, the D layer disappears and the F1 and F2 layers collapse into a single F layer.

The **grey line or terminator** is the portion of the Earth where the sunlit part of the atmosphere meets the dark portion. In other words, the grey line is found wherever dusk or dawn occurs. Lower frequencies have enhanced propagation on the grey line along Northwest and Southeast bearings. People can use directional antennas and orient them to be able to take advantage of the grey line. Along the grey line, the D layer rapidly dissipates, so operators don't necessarily have to propagate along the grey line to reap the benefits of reduced absorption by the D layer.

Critical Angle and Frequency

In amateur radio, the **incident angle** refers to the angle from which an RF signal travels away from the transmitting antenna and hits the ionosphere. The **critical angle** is the greatest angle at which a transmitter can send a signal that will still return it to Earth. The critical angle depends on ionospheric conditions. It's possible to have an angle that is too steep to be refracted or a signal that experiences minor refraction but still mostly travels into space.

HF Scatter

Skywaves allow communication beyond the line of sight. "**Skip**" refers to the phenomenon of skywaves bouncing between Earth and the upper atmosphere to travel between stations. When a skywave requires more than one "skip" to reach its destination, it's called multi-hop propagation. **Multi-hop propagation** allows signals to transmit across much further distances.

Distortions happen when signals are scattered into a skip zone through various radio transmission paths. A **skip zone** is a reception dead zone, meaning a place where communications stations cannot receive transmissions by skywave or groundwave propagation.

Subelement G3 – Radio Wave Propagation

HF signals in the skip zone are weak because only a little of the radio transmission is scattered into the skip zone. Scatter allows signals to be heard in the skip zone. **Scatter signals** have a fluttering sound and often sound distorted because energy is scattered into the skip zones through several different radio wave paths (i.e., **multipath distortion**).

Near Vertical Incidence Skywave

A **Near Vertical Incidence Skywave (NVIS)** refers to an antenna technology that generates a type of skywave that makes it possible to communicate with skip zones and transmit over rocky terrain. NVIS requires antennas that can transmit at steep angles, greater than 75 degrees, over lower HF channels. Generally, NVIS transmits over a limited range (between 2 and 10 MHz).

Since the incident angle determines a signal's range, lower incident angles allow transmissions to travel further. For NVIS, the incident angle sends signals almost straight up towards the ionosphere, so they bounce back down relatively close to the origination point (transmitter). For this reason, short-distance MF or HF transmissions through difficult terrain rely on high elevation angles used in NVIS propagation.

NVIS has less attenuation than most skywave propagation because these signals take a more direct (quicker) route when passing through the D layer; therefore, they reach the F layer faster. Also, since the signal lands close to the transmitter, geologic heterogeneity does not reduce the signal's strength as much. Finally, fewer multipath signals can be incorporated with the transmission, which causes less echo and reduction in signal quality overall. NVIS coverage is omnidirectional, so azimuth, or directional orientation, is less critical.

NVIS antennas are erected close to the ground and typically installed between 1/10 and ¼ wavelength high. Since NVIS has poor gain at the groundwave level, signals are less susceptible to **radio direction finding (RDF)** operations and **signal jamming**. NVIS does not require much power, so it works well for ad hoc scenarios – like military operations and emergency relief – that require portability and flexibility.

Communicating with NVIS requires both transmitters and receivers to have NVIS antennas. Typically, operators use **NVIS dipoles**, which differ from standard HF dipoles. To construct a NVIS dipole, amateurs adapt a normal HF half-wave dipole to 0.2 wavelengths above the ground as opposed to regular HF dipoles, which are usually 0.5 wavelengths above the ground. Lower optimal height is required when the ground has a higher conductivity. Adapting the antenna in this manner transmits a steeper radiation angle.

There are also many alternative NVIS antenna types for hams looking to expand beyond the dipole. Operators can use field expedient antennas, an inverted vee, an unbalanced wire, or vehicle-mounted, fixed site applications like conical spiral and vertical log periodic antennas.

Subelement G3 – Questions

G3A

1. How does a higher sunspot number affect HF propagation?
    a. Higher sunspot numbers generally indicate a greater probability of good propagation at higher frequencies
    b. Lower sunspot numbers generally indicate greater probability of sporadic E propagation
    c. A zero sunspot number indicates that radio propagation is not possible on any band
    d. A zero sunspot number indicates undisturbed conditions

2. What effect does a sudden ionospheric disturbance have on the daytime ionospheric propagation?
    a. It enhances propagation on all HF frequencies
    b. It disrupts signals on lower frequencies more than those on higher frequencies
    c. It disrupts communications via satellite more than direct communications
    d. None, because only areas on the night side of the Earth are affected

3. Approximately how long does it take for the increased ultraviolet and X-ray radiation from a solar flare to affect radio propagation on Earth?
    a. 28 days
    b. 1 to 2 hours
    c. 8 minutes
    d. 20 to 40 hours

4. Which of the following are the least reliable bands for long-distance communications during periods of low solar activity?
    a. 80 meters and 160 meters
    b. 60 meters and 40 meters
    c. 30 meters and 20 meters
    d. 15 meters, 12 meters, and 10 meters

5. What is the solar flux index?
    a. A measure of the highest frequency that is useful for ionospheric propagation between two points on Earth
    b. A count of sunspots that is adjusted for solar emissions
    c. Another name for the American sunspot number
    d. A measure of solar radiation with a wavelength of 10.7 centimeters

6. What is a geomagnetic storm?
    a. A sudden drop in the solar flux index
    b. A thunderstorm that affects radio propagation
    c. Ripples in the geomagnetic force
    d. A temporary disturbance in Earth's geomagnetic field

Subelement G3 – Questions

7. At what point in the solar cycle does the 20-meter band usually support worldwide propagation during daylight hours?
   a. At the summer solstice
   b. Only at the maximum point
   c. Only at the minimum point
   d. At any point

8. How can a geomagnetic storm affect HF propagation?
   a. Improve high-latitude HF propagation
   b. Degrade ground wave propagation
   c. Improve ground wave propagation
   d. Degrade high-latitude HF propagation

9. How can high geomagnetic activity benefit radio communications?
   a. Creates auroras that can reflect VHF signals
   b. Increases signal strength for HF signals passing through the polar regions
   c. Improve HF long path propagation
   d. Reduce long delayed echoes

10. What causes HF propagation conditions to vary periodically in a 26- to 28-day cycle?
    a. Long term oscillations in the upper atmosphere
    b. Cyclic variation in Earth's radiation belts
    c. Rotation of the Sun's surface layers around its axis
    d. The position of the Moon in its orbit

11. How long does it take a coronal mass ejection to affect radio propagation on Earth?
    a. 28 days
    b. 14 days
    c. 4 to 8 minutes
    d. 15 hours to several days

12. What does the K-index measure?
    a. The relative position of sunspots on the surface of the Sun
    b. The short-term stability of Earth's geomagnetic field
    c. The short-term stability of the Sun's magnetic field
    d. The solar radio flux at Boulder, Colorado

13. What does the A-index measure?
    a. The relative position of sunspots on the surface of the Sun
    b. The amount of polarization of the Sun's electric field
    c. The long-term stability of Earth's geomagnetic field
    d. The solar radio flux at Boulder, Colorado

14. How is long distance radio communication usually affected by the charged particles that reach Earth from solar coronal holes?
    a. HF communication is improved
    b. HF communication is disturbed
    c. VHF/UHF ducting is improved
    d. VHF/UHF ducting is disturbed

G3B

1. What is a characteristic of skywave signals arriving at your location by both short-path and long-path propagation?
    a. Periodic fading approximately every 10 seconds
    b. Signal strength increased by 3 dB
    c. The signal might be cancelled causing severe attenuation
    d. A slightly delayed echo might be heard

2. What factors affect the MUF?
    a. Path distance and location
    b. Time of day and season
    c. Solar radiation and ionospheric disturbances
    d. All these choices are correct

3. Which frequency will have the least attenuation for long-distance skip propagation?
    a. Just below the MUF
    b. Just above the LUF
    c. Just below the critical frequency
    d. Just above the critical frequency

4. Which of the following is a way to determine current propagation on a desired band from your station?
    a. Use a network of automated receiving stations on the internet to see where your transmissions are being received
    b. Check the A-index
    c. Send a series of dots and listen for echoes
    d. All these choices are correct

5. How does the ionosphere affect radio waves with frequencies below the MUF and above the LUF?
    a. They are refracted back to Earth
    b. They pass through the ionosphere
    c. They are amplified by interaction with the ionosphere
    d. They are refracted and trapped in the ionosphere to circle Earth

6. What usually happens to radio waves with frequencies below the LUF?
    a. They are refracted back to Earth
    b. They pass through the ionosphere
    c. They are attenuated before reaching the destination
    d. They are refracted and trapped in the ionosphere to circle Earth

7. What does LUF stand for?
    a. The Lowest Usable Frequency for communications between two specific points
    b. Lowest Usable Frequency for communications to any point outside a 100-mile radius
    c. The Lowest Usable Frequency during a 24-hour period
    d. Lowest Usable Frequency during the past 60 minutes

Subelement G3 – Questions

8. What does MUF stand for?
    a. The Minimum Usable Frequency for communications between two points
    b. The Maximum Usable Frequency for communications between two points
    c. The Minimum Usable Frequency during a 24-hour period
    d. The Maximum Usable Frequency during a 24-hour period

9. What is the approximate maximum distance along the Earth's surface normally covered in one hop using the F2 region?
    a. 180 miles
    b. 1,200 miles
    c. 2,500 miles
    d. 12,000 miles

10. What is the approximate maximum distance along the Earth's surface normally covered in one hop using the E region?
    a. 180 miles
    b. 1,200 miles
    c. 2,500 miles
    d. 12,000 miles

11. What happens to HF propagation when the LUF exceeds the MUF?
    a. Propagation via ordinary skywave communications is not possible over that path
    b. HF communications over the path are enhanced
    c. Double-hop propagation along the path is more common
    d. Propagation over the path on all HF frequencies is enhanced

12. Which of the following is typical of the lower HF frequencies during the summer?
    a. Poor propagation at any time of day
    b. World-wide propagation during daylight hours
    c. Heavy distortion on signals due to photon absorption
    d. High levels of atmospheric noise or static

G3C

1. Which ionospheric region is closest to the surface of Earth?
    a. The D region
    b. The E region
    c. The F1 region
    d. The F2 region

2. What is meant by the term "critical frequency" at a given incidence angle?
    a. The highest frequency which is refracted back to Earth
    b. The lowest frequency which is refracted back to Earth
    c. The frequency at which the signal-to-noise ratio approaches unity
    d. The frequency at which the signal-to-noise ratio is 6 dB

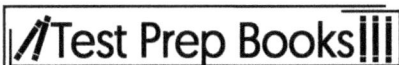

Subelement G3 – Questions

3. Why is skip propagation via the F2 region longer than that via the other ionospheric regions?
   a. Because it is the densest
   b. Because of the Doppler effect
   c. Because it is the highest
   d. Because of temperature inversions

4. What does the term "critical angle" mean, as applied to radio wave propagation?
   a. The long path azimuth of a distant station
   b. The short path azimuth of a distant station
   c. The lowest takeoff angle that will return a radio wave to Earth under specific ionospheric conditions
   d. The highest takeoff angle that will return a radio wave to Earth under specific ionospheric conditions

5. Why is long-distance communication on the 40-, 60-, 80-, and 160-meter bands more difficult during the day?
   a. The F region absorbs signals at these frequencies during daylight hours
   b. The F region is unstable during daylight hours
   c. The D region absorbs signals at these frequencies during daylight hours
   d. The E region is unstable during daylight hours

6. What is a characteristic of HF scatter?
   a. Phone signals have high intelligibility
   b. Signals have a fluttering sound
   c. There are very large, sudden swings in signal strength
   d. Scatter propagation occurs only at night

7. What makes HF scatter signals often sound distorted?
   a. The ionospheric region involved is unstable
   b. Ground waves are absorbing much of the signal
   c. The E region is not present
   d. Energy is scattered into the skip zone through several different paths

8. Why are HF scatter signals in the skip zone usually weak?
   a. Only a small part of the signal energy is scattered into the skip zone
   b. Signals are scattered from the magnetosphere, which is not a good reflector
   c. Propagation is via ground waves, which absorb most of the signal energy
   d. Propagation is via ducts in the F region, which absorb most of the energy

9. What type of propagation allows signals to be heard in the transmitting station's skip zone?
   a. Faraday rotation
   b. Scatter
   c. Chordal hop
   d. Short path

Subelement G3 – Questions

10. What is near vertical incidence skywave (NVIS) propagation?
    a. Propagation near the MUF
    b. Short distance MF or HF propagation at high elevation angles
    c. Long path HF propagation at sunrise and sunset
    d. Double hop propagation near the LUF

11. Which ionospheric region is the most absorbent of signals below 10 MHz during daylight hours?
    a. The F2 region
    b. The F1 region
    c. The E region
    d. The D region

Subelement G3 – Answer Explanations

G3A

1. A	8. D
2. B	9. A
3. C	10. C
4. D	11. D
5. D	12. B
6. D	13. C
7. D	14. B

G3B

1. D	7. A
2. D	8. B
3. A	9. C
4. A	10. B
5. A	11. A
6. C	12. D

G3C

1. A	7. D
2. A	8. A
3. C	9. B
4. D	10. B
5. C	11. D
6. B	

Subelement G4 – Amateur Radio Practices

G4A

Station Configuration and Setup

All stations need certain equipment to function properly. Three pieces of equipment form the core of all amateur radio stations: a transceiver, an antenna, and a power supply. A **transceiver** is the centerpiece of the station and allows communication on VHF and UHF frequencies. The **antenna** is necessary to transmit and receive radio signals, and can range from smaller, easier-to-move mobile antennas to a large Yagi beam antenna. The amount of power needed from the **power supply** often depends on the setup, but can range from as low as 5 W or less to as high as the legal limit of 1500 W.

Whatever equipment you decide on, make sure to consider the space your station is set up in and provide courtesy for others. The space where you set up your station should have enough room to set up all your equipment and antennas comfortably and have access to the necessary power supply. Test the setup to see if electrical noise from nearby devices causes interference with your antenna; move your antenna further away if necessary. Additionally, if your station is a home station, try to set it up in a place that won't cause issues with other members of the house; a setup in the middle of the main room will be distracting to everyone, including yourself!

When communicating with others over amateur radio, it is generally considered polite to keep your messages as brief as possible. Practice being concise but clear with your messages. Taking too long to deliver your message often annoys other amateur radio operators, especially more experienced ones or ones involved in competitions that involve many quick communications from lots of people. Imagine you are talking to someone who has hundreds of people trying to talk to them and is trying to respond to as many as possible. You don't want to waste their time, or they may ignore you in the future. Keep messages to the point and practice enunciation to avoid having to send too many repeat messages. Some of the most important information you can relay in your first message to a station is your callsign, your location, and the callsign of who you are calling to verify you have the right station.

In addition to memorizing your callsign, you may also want to memorize several common **Q signals**. **Q signals** are shorthand for a variety of common questions or replies and often need to be expressed quickly and concisely. For example, QRH is used to ask if your frequency varies, or to reply to someone asking QRH that their frequency does vary. QRO asks if you should increase power or replies to someone asking QRO that they should increase power. Q signals are questions if they are followed by a question mark; otherwise, they are statements. There are a lot of Q signals, so it's best to memorize the common ones that may come up often.

Proper equipment maintenance is also important. Make sure you have all the necessary tools, such as wire cutters, soldering irons, multimeters, and more. Check which parts you may need spares for, like screws or connectors. Purchase any necessary adapters for audio, power, and RF cables to make sure you don't have any issues replacing cables. Since amateur radio uses a lot of electrical components, standard electrical safety parts, such as electrical tape and spare fuses, are also helpful. Soft brushes and cans of compressed air or other solvents help keep parts clean and prevent or slow corrosion.

G4B

Test and Monitoring Equipment

To make sure your station is in good working order and to perform periodic maintenance checks, you should own or consider owning certain pieces of radio and electrical testing equipment. A **multimeter** is an essential electrical testing tool that allows you to measure voltage, current, and resistance. A high-quality multimeter may also have functions like continuity testing. Multimeters allow you to test a variety of elements of your station setup, such as making sure power connections are correctly drawing the right amount of voltage and current. They can also help you troubleshoot any issues that arise later.

Other useful testing equipment includes the following:

Power meters monitor the power usage of your equipment and are essential for making sure you are getting the most out of your antennas and transmitters.

An **inductance-capacitance (L-C) meter** allows you to measure inductance and capacitance values of a circuit. Some multimeters may have a similar function, but a dedicated L-C meter is much more precise.

A **nano vector network analyzer (VNA)** is a special device that combines many functions together in a single test set. It can test antennas for impedance, or test individual or sets of components like inductors and capacitors all in one device.

G4C

Interference to Consumer Electronics

The signals that come from amateur radio stations can cause interference with a variety of consumer electronics like TVs, radios, and phones. Cordless phones use radio signals and have no protection from such interference. This interference only happens when the radio station is in active use, so this interference may not always be apparent. Consider how to alter your setup to minimize this interference—usually, you want to move the radio station further away from the devices being interfered with. This is especially important when setting up an amateur radio station in a very populated area like a residential neighborhood. Taller antennas can help get your radio signals up and over the devices, which minimizes or removes the interference, but they may be subject to housing code or simply may not look appealing in your neighborhood. Be considerate of how your radio station can interfere with consumer electronics and take the necessary steps during station setup to avoid it as much as possible.

Grounding and Bonding

Amateur radio stations can use current and voltages that are potentially dangerous to a person, equipment, or building, and they can also cause electrical interference with audio equipment. The National Electrical Code is the United States' regulation standard for electrical installations, so you should either familiarize yourself with it or work with a licensed electrician when installing necessary power components for your station setup. To provide an electrical overload, your station equipment should be connected to a rod that is at least eight feet long and driven entirely into the ground. This method of **grounding** the circuit diverts all excess electricity in your setup into the ground and safely

Subelement G4 – Amateur Radio Practices

disperses it. Grounding is one of the most effective things you can do to minimize electrical dangers with your setup.

Another major safety step you can take is **bonding** your equipment. Bonding involves connecting components that aren't intended to carry a current. While this may seem counterintuitive, if the bonded pathways also lead to a grounding point, bonding effectively helps disperse electrical surges into the grounding path. This is especially useful if a person touches two metal parts that are part of an electrical fault and inadvertently creates an electrical pathway through themselves for the current, which is extremely dangerous. Bonding all your equipment—in other words, connecting all the components that aren't intended to carry a current and then connecting that to the grounding path—is an important way to keep safe in an electricity-heavy setup like an amateur radio station.

G4D

Speech Processors

Amateur radio is a way for individuals to communicate with each other using radio signals. However, the human voice itself usually does not transmit well through radio signals because the average power is small compared to the peak power. Human speech waveforms naturally have peaks and valleys to them, but the valleys are so much lower that it drags the average power down, and a consistent average power is more important for the radio signal. To solve this, **speech processors** are used to help increase the average power and make the waveform average more consistent. The diagram below shows an example of this difference:

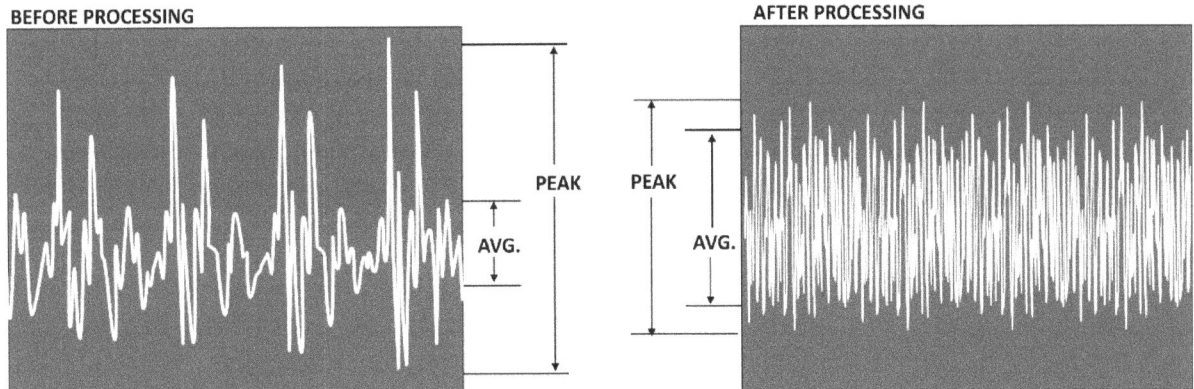

Speech processors can be a device or software, but the general concept is the same regardless of the form. Speech processing is the act of averaging out the level of power in the waveform of human speech to make it clearer, more consistent, and better suited for radio signals. However, since this works by increasing the lower end of the waveform to be closer to the peaks, the overall low end of the audio is increased. This can lead to more noticeable background noise during communication. Speech-processed signals can also draw more power from the transmitter. If your radio station setup doesn't have proper temperature control, the transmitter can begin overheating. An overheating transmitter can be easily damaged, so you may need to reduce either the power of the speech processing or the power of the transmitter as a whole.

Speech processing enhances the low end of an audio signal and cannot increase the peak of the signal, which means it cannot increase the actual volume of a signal. It is also technically a distortion of an

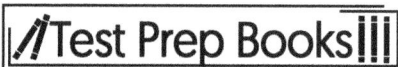

Subelement G4 – Amateur Radio Practices

audio signal, which makes the signal less natural at the receiving end. If you have good propagation and a clear signal to begin with, speech processing would be unnecessary. Try to avoid using speech processing, or at least only use the minimum amount of speech processing necessary for your message to be understood by the receiving station.

S Meters

In addition to your own outgoing signal, consider the quality of incoming signals to your station. This is where a device called an **S meter** comes in. S meters use a scale from S1 to S9 to describe the strength of an incoming signal. The higher the S reading, the stronger the signal. S meters do have some quirks to be aware of. They work by measuring the voltage passing through the automatic gain control (AGC) circuitry. Thus, two S meters may give slightly or even completely different readings. S meters are best used to measure the strength of signals relative to each other, whereas simply listening to the audio output may not make it obvious. For example, an incoming signal may first arrive as an S7 and then adjust to an S9, but the audio output of the signal sounds nearly identical to the human ear. In this case, an S meter allows you to more easily observe that the signal strength has improved, since it directly measures voltage passing through the system to give its readings.

Sideband Operation Near Band Edges

To understand sidebands, visualize a car driving through a tunnel. The car's width means it cannot go too far left or right, or it will collide with the walls of the tunnel. Radio frequencies have a similar principle when transmitting – their **sidebands**. Essentially, radio signals have a "width" to the range of frequency space they use, and you need to keep this in mind to make sure you are operating only within your permitted range. You may need to check your transmitter's instruction manual to understand how your sidebands are configured, but there is usually a range to be aware of. For example, a transmitter may say that the **upper side band (USB)** and **lower side band (LSB)** have a range of 3 kHz. This means that whatever the frequency is displayed on the radio, it can be observed at a range of up to 3 kHz above or below that frequency. Federal regulations require that amateur radio stations only operate within specified frequency ranges depending on their license type and operating mode, so make sure you are aware of the upper and lower limits to your broadcasting—in other words, don't drive too close to the wall of the tunnel!

G4E

Mobile and Portable HF Radio Stations

Not all radio stations are big setups that take up a whole desk's worth of space and have large antennas. As technology has improved, radio setups have become more mobile, allowing for smaller and more compact station setups. Mobile transceivers may be the size of a book, and some are even the size of a handheld device. These smaller devices may have slightly different sources of a suitable power supply or may even be battery powered. Modern devices may have a built-in antenna or connect to a small mobile antenna. Mobile and fully portable transceivers can be extremely useful for communications in remote areas and situations such as mountainous or heavily forested terrain.

Alternative Energy Source Operation

In emergency situations, one of the strongest advantages of amateur radio is that radio signals require little infrastructure compared to telephone lines or internet cables. However, these devices all still require power, and in an extreme scenario your normal power source may be unavailable; perhaps power lines are down or broken. Thus, in emergency situations, it can be extremely important for your radio station setup to have an alternative power source. As long as the power is converted into the necessary power supply for the transmitter and devices to function, any suitable alternative energy source can work. Solar and wind power are renewable sources of power, and portable generators are a classic backup solution. However, a serious disaster could render all these options unavailable, so the final fallback is battery power. Many radios can operate with roughly 12 volts of power, so a standard 12-volt battery is enough to run a standard setup. Keep the power draw and battery capacity of this emergency setup in mind to avoid running out of power at a critical moment.

Subelement G4 – Questions

G4A

1. What is the purpose of the notch filter found on many HF transceivers?
    A. To restrict the transmitter voice bandwidth
    B. To reduce interference from carriers in the receiver passband
    C. To eliminate receiver interference from impulse noise sources
    D. To remove interfering splatter generated by signals on adjacent frequencies

2. What is the benefit of using the opposite or "reverse" sideband when receiving CW?
    A. Interference from impulse noise will be eliminated
    B. More stations can be accommodated within a given signal passband
    C. It may be possible to reduce or eliminate interference from other signals
    D. Accidental out-of-band operation can be prevented

3. How does a noise blanker work?
    A. By temporarily increasing received bandwidth
    B. By redirecting noise pulses into a filter capacitor
    C. By reducing receiver gain during a noise pulse
    D. By clipping noise peaks

4. What is the effect on plate current of the correct setting of a vacuum-tube RF power amplifier's TUNE control?
    A. A pronounced peak
    B. A pronounced dip
    C. No change will be observed
    D. A slow, rhythmic oscillation

5. Why is automatic level control (ALC) used with an RF power amplifier?
    A. To balance the transmitter audio frequency response
    B. To reduce harmonic radiation
    C. To prevent excessive drive
    D. To increase overall efficiency

6. What is the purpose of an antenna tuner?
    A. Reduce the SWR in the feed line to the antenna
    B. Reduce the power dissipation in the feedline to the antenna
    C. Increase power transfer from the transmitter to the feed line
    D. All these choices are correct

7. What happens as a receiver's noise reduction control level is increased?
    A. Received signals may become distorted
    B. Received frequency may become unstable
    C. CW signals may become severely attenuated
    D. Received frequency may shift several kHz

Subelement G4 – Amateur Radio Practices

8. What is the correct adjustment for the LOAD or COUPLING control of a vacuum tube RF power amplifier?
    A. Minimum SWR on the antenna
    B. Minimum plate current without exceeding maximum allowable grid current
    C. Highest plate voltage while minimizing grid current
    D. Desired power output without exceeding maximum allowable plate current

9. What is the purpose of delaying RF output after activating a transmitter's keying line to an external amplifier?
    A. To prevent key clicks on CW
    B. To prevent transient overmodulation
    C. To allow time for the amplifier to switch the antenna between the transceiver and the amplifier output
    D. To allow time for the amplifier power supply to reach operating level

10. What is the function of an electronic keyer?
    A. Automatic transmit/receive switching
    B. Automatic generation of dots and dashes for CW operation
    C. To allow time for switching the antenna from the receiver to the transmitter
    D. Computer interface for PSK and RTTY operation

11. Why should the ALC system be inactive when transmitting AFSK data signals?
    A. ALC will invert the modulation of the AFSK mode
    B. The ALC action distorts the signal
    C. When using digital modes, too much ALC activity can cause the transmitter to overheat
    D. All these choices are correct

12. Which of the following is a common use of the dual-VFO feature on a transceiver?
    A. To allow transmitting on two frequencies at once
    B. To permit full duplex operation -- that is, transmitting and receiving at the same time
    C. To transmit on one frequency and listen on another
    D. To improve frequency accuracy by allowing variable frequency output (VFO) operation

13. What is the purpose of using a receive attenuator?
    A. To prevent receiver overload from strong incoming signals
    B. To reduce the transmitter power when driving a linear amplifier
    C. To reduce power consumption when operating from batteries
    D. To reduce excessive audio level on strong signals

G4B

1. What item of test equipment contains horizontal and vertical channel amplifiers?
    A. An ohmmeter
    B. A signal generator
    C. An ammeter
    D. An oscilloscope

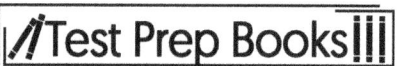

Subelement G4 – Amateur Radio Practices

2. Which of the following is an advantage of an oscilloscope versus a digital voltmeter?
   A. An oscilloscope uses less power
   B. Complex impedances can be easily measured
   C. Greater precision
   D. Complex waveforms can be measured

3. Which of the following is the best instrument to use for checking the keying waveform of a CW transmitter?
   A. An oscilloscope
   B. A field strength meter
   C. A sidetone monitor
   D. A wavemeter

4. What signal source is connected to the vertical input of an oscilloscope when checking the RF envelope pattern of a transmitted signal?
   A. The local oscillator of the transmitter
   B. An external RF oscillator
   C. The transmitter balanced mixer output
   D. The attenuated RF output of the transmitter

5. Why do voltmeters have high input impedance?
   A. It improves the frequency response
   B. It allows for higher voltages to be safely measured
   C. It improves the resolution of the readings
   D. It decreases the loading on circuits being measured

6. What is an advantage of a digital multimeter as compared to an analog multimeter?
   A. Better for measuring computer circuits
   B. Less prone to overload
   C. Higher precision
   D. Faster response

7. What signals are used to conduct a two-tone test?
   A. Two audio signals of the same frequency shifted 90 degrees
   B. Two non-harmonically related audio signals
   C. Two swept frequency tones
   D. Two audio frequency range square wave signals of equal amplitude

8. What transmitter performance parameter does a two-tone test analyze?
   A. Linearity
   B. Percentage of suppression of the carrier and undesired sideband for SSB
   C. Percentage of frequency modulation
   D. Percentage of carrier phase shift

9. When is an analog multimeter preferred to a digital multimeter?
   A. When testing logic circuits
   B. When high precision is desired
   C. When measuring the frequency of an oscillator
   D. When adjusting circuits for maximum or minimum values

84

10. Which of the following can be determined with a directional wattmeter?
    A. Standing wave ratio
    B. Antenna front-to-back ratio
    C. RF interference
    D. Radio wave propagation

11. Which of the following must be connected to an antenna analyzer when it is being used for SWR measurements?
    A. Receiver
    B. Transmitter
    C. Antenna and feed line
    D. All these choices are correct

12. What effect can strong signals from nearby transmitters have on an antenna analyzer?
    A. Desensitization which can cause intermodulation products which interfere with impedance readings
    B. Received power that interferes with SWR readings
    C. Generation of harmonics which interfere with frequency readings
    D. All these choices are correct

13. Which of the following can be measured with an antenna analyzer?
    A. Front-to-back ratio of an antenna
    B. Power output from a transmitter
    C. Impedance of coaxial cable
    D. Gain of a directional antenna

G4C

1. Which of the following might be useful in reducing RF interference to audio frequency circuits?
    A. Bypass inductor
    B. Bypass capacitor
    C. Forward-biased diode
    D. Reverse-biased diode

2. Which of the following could be a cause of interference covering a wide range of frequencies?
    A. Not using a balun or line isolator to feed balanced antennas
    B. Lack of rectification of the transmitter's signal in power conductors
    C. Arcing at a poor electrical connection
    D. Using a balun to feed an unbalanced antenna

3. What sound is heard from an audio device experiencing RF interference from a single sideband phone transmitter?
    A. A steady hum whenever the transmitter is on the air
    B. On-and-off humming or clicking
    C. Distorted speech
    D. Clearly audible speech

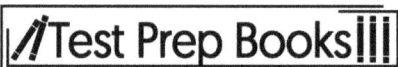

Subelement G4 – Amateur Radio Practices

4. What sound is heard from an audio device experiencing RF interference from a CW transmitter?
   A. On-and-off humming or clicking
   B. A CW signal at a nearly pure audio frequency
   C. A chirpy CW signal
   D. Severely distorted audio

5. What is a possible cause of high voltages that produce RF burns?
   A. Flat braid rather than round wire has been used for the ground wire
   B. Insulated wire has been used for the ground wire
   C. The ground rod is resonant
   D. The ground wire has high impedance on that frequency

6. What is a possible effect of a resonant ground connection?
   A. Overheating of ground straps
   B. Corrosion of the ground rod
   C. High RF voltages on the enclosures of station equipment
   D. A ground loop

7. Why should soldered joints not be used in lightning protection ground connections?
   A. A soldered joint will likely be destroyed by the heat of a lightning strike
   B. Solder flux will prevent a low conductivity connection
   C. Solder has too high a dielectric constant to provide adequate lightning protection
   D. All these choices are correct

8. Which of the following would reduce RF interference caused by common-mode current on an audio cable?
   A. Place a ferrite choke on the cable
   B. Connect the center conductor to the shield of all cables to short circuit the RFI signal
   C. Ground the center conductor of the audio cable causing the interference
   D. Add an additional insulating jacket to the cable

9. How can the effects of ground loops be minimized?
   A. Connect all ground conductors in series
   B. Connect the AC neutral conductor to the ground wire
   C. Avoid using lock washers and star washers when making ground connections
   D. Bond equipment enclosures together

10. What could be a symptom caused by a ground loop in your station's audio connections?
    A. You receive reports of "hum" on your station's transmitted signal
    B. The SWR reading for one or more antennas is suddenly very high
    C. An item of station equipment starts to draw excessive amounts of current
    D. You receive reports of harmonic interference from your station

11. What technique helps to minimize RF "hot spots" in an amateur station?
    A. Building all equipment in a metal enclosure
    B. Using surge suppressor power outlets
    C. Bonding all equipment enclosures together
    D. Placing low-pass filters on all feed lines

12. Why must all metal enclosures of station equipment be grounded?
    A. It prevents a blown fuse in the event of an internal short circuit
    B. It prevents signal overload
    C. It ensures that the neutral wire is grounded
    D. It ensures that hazardous voltages cannot appear on the chassis

G4D

1. What is the purpose of a speech processor in a transceiver?
    A. Increase the apparent loudness of transmitted voice signals
    B. Increase transmitter bass response for more natural-sounding SSB signals
    C. Prevent distortion of voice signals
    D. Decrease high-frequency voice output to prevent out-of-band operation

2. How does a speech processor affect a single sideband phone signal?
    A. It increases peak power
    B. It increases average power
    C. It reduces harmonic distortion
    D. It reduces intermodulation distortion

3. What is the effect of an incorrectly adjusted speech processor?
    A. Distorted speech
    B. Excess intermodulation products
    C. Excessive background noise
    D. All these choices are correct

4. What does an S meter measure?
    A. Carrier suppression
    B. Impedance
    C. Received signal strength
    D. Transmitter power output

5. How does a signal that reads 20 dB over S9 compare to one that reads S9 on a receiver, assuming a properly calibrated S meter?
    A. It is 10 times less powerful
    B. It is 20 times less powerful
    C. It is 20 times more powerful
    D. It is 100 times more powerful

6. How much change in signal strength is typically represented by one S unit?
    A. 6 dB
    B. 12 dB
    C. 15 dB
    D. 18 dB

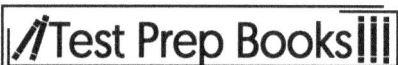

Subelement G4 – Amateur Radio Practices

7. How much must the power output of a transmitter be raised to change the S meter reading on a distant receiver from S8 to S9?
   A. Approximately 1.5 times
   B. Approximately 2 times
   C. Approximately 4 times
   D. Approximately 8 times

8. What frequency range is occupied by a 3 kHz LSB signal when the displayed carrier frequency is set to 7.178 MHz?
   A. 7.178 MHz to 7.181 MHz
   B. 7.178 MHz to 7.184 MHz
   C. 7.175 MHz to 7.178 MHz
   D. 7.1765 MHz to 7.1795 MHz

9. What frequency range is occupied by a 3 kHz USB signal with the displayed carrier frequency set to 14.347 MHz?
   A. 14.347 MHz to 14.647 MHz
   B. 14.347 MHz to 14.350 MHz
   C. 14.344 MHz to 14.347 MHz
   D. 14.3455 MHz to 14.3485 MHz

10. How close to the lower edge of a band's phone segment should your displayed carrier frequency be when using a 3 kHz wide LSB?
    A. At least 3 kHz above the edge of the segment
    B. At least 3 kHz below the edge of the segment
    C. At least 1 kHz below the edge of the segment
    D. At least 1 kHz above the edge of the segment

11. How close to the upper edge of a band's phone segment should your displayed carrier frequency be when using a 3 kHz wide USB?
    A. At least 3 kHz above the edge of the band
    B. At least 3 kHz below the edge of the band
    C. At least 1 kHz above the edge of the segment
    D. At least 1 kHz below the edge of the segment

G4E

1. What is the purpose of a capacitance hat on a mobile antenna?
   A. To increase the power handling capacity of a whip antenna
   B. To reduce radiation resistance
   C. To electrically lengthen a physically short antenna
   D. To lower the radiation angle

2. What is the purpose of a corona ball on an HF mobile antenna?
   A. To narrow the operating bandwidth of the antenna
   B. To increase the "Q" of the antenna
   C. To reduce the chance of damage if the antenna should strike an object
   D. To reduce RF voltage discharge from the tip of the antenna while transmitting

3. Which of the following direct, fused power connections would be the best for a 100-watt HF mobile installation?
- A. To the battery using heavy-gauge wire
- B. To the alternator or generator using heavy-gauge wire
- C. To the battery using insulated heavy duty balanced transmission line
- D. To the alternator or generator using insulated heavy duty balanced transmission line

4. Why should DC power for a 100-watt HF transceiver not be supplied by a vehicle's auxiliary power socket?
- A. The socket is not wired with an RF-shielded power cable
- B. The socket's wiring may be inadequate for the current drawn by the transceiver
- C. The DC polarity of the socket is reversed from the polarity of modern HF transceivers
- D. Drawing more than 50 watts from this socket could cause the engine to overheat

5. Which of the following most limits an HF mobile installation?
- A. "Picket fencing"
- B. The wire gauge of the DC power line to the transceiver
- C. Efficiency of the electrically short antenna
- D. FCC rules limiting mobile output power on the 75-meter band

6. What is one disadvantage of using a shortened mobile antenna as opposed to a full-size antenna?
- A. Short antennas are more likely to cause distortion of transmitted signals
- B. Q of the antenna will be very low
- C. Operating bandwidth may be very limited
- D. Harmonic radiation may increase

7. Which of the following may cause receive interference to an HF transceiver installed in a vehicle?
- A. The battery charging system
- B. The fuel delivery system
- C. The control computers
- D. All these choices are correct

8. In what configuration are the individual cells in a solar panel connected together?
- A. Series-parallel
- B. Shunt
- C. Bypass
- D. Full-wave bridge

9. What is the approximate open-circuit voltage from a fully illuminated silicon photovoltaic cell?
- A. 0.02 VDC
- B. 0.5 VDC
- C. 0.2 VDC
- D. 1.38 VDC

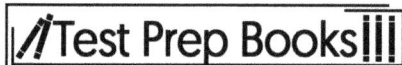

10. Why should a series diode be connected between a solar panel and a storage battery that is being charged by the panel?
    A. To prevent overload by regulating the charging voltage
    B. To prevent discharge of the battery through the panel during times of low or no illumination
    C. To limit the current flowing from the panel to a safe value
    D. To prevent damage to the battery due to excessive voltage at high illumination levels

11. What precaution should be taken when connecting a solar panel to a lithium iron phosphate battery?
    A. Ground the solar panel outer metal framework
    B. Ensure the battery is placed terminals-up
    C. A series resistor must be in place
    D. The solar panel must have a charge controller

Subelement G4 – Answer Key

G4A

1. B	8. D
2. C	9. C
3. C	10. B
4. B	11. B
5. C	12. C
6. C	13. A
7. A	

G4B

1. D	8. A
2. D	9. D
3. A	10. A
4. D	11. C
5. D	12. B
6. C	13. C
7. B	

G4C

1. B	7. A
2. C	8. A
3. C	9. D
4. A	10. A
5. D	11. C
6. C	12. D

G4D

1. A	7. C
2. B	8. C
3. D	9. B
4. C	10. A
5. D	11. B
6. A	

G4E

1. C	7. D
2. D	8. A
3. A	9. B
4. B	10. B
5. C	11. D
6. C	

Subelement G5 – Electrical Principles

G5A

Reactance

Reactance is a trait of electrical circuits and shares similarities with resistance, though there are several key differences. Reactance is a measure of how much opposition there is to an alternating current. This opposition is usually generated by inductance, capacitance, or other factors. Since it is an opposing force to voltage, it is like resistance and is also measured in ohms. Positive values indicate inductive reactance, and negative values indicate capacitive reactance. Unlike resistance, which applies a constant resisting force to the circuit, reactance adapts based on the frequency of the alternating current. As frequency increases, inductive reactance increases in strength and capacitive reactance decreases in strength. Reactance also does not dissipate the electrical energy as heat, but instead momentarily stores the energy before releasing it one quarter-cycle later.

Inductance

Conductive materials have a trait called **inductance**, which is a measure of how easily that material accepts a change in electrical current. While the comparison is not perfect, think of a heavy object and how much that object resists any attempts to move it. Inductance is then defined as a ratio between the strength of the induced voltage that is opposing the change in current compared to the rate of change of the current in the circuit that is causing the induced voltage. Components in circuits designed to cause inductance are called inductors, and inductance itself is measured in a unit called the henry (H), equivalent to the amount of inductance causing one volt against a current changing at one amp per second.

Capacitance

Capacitance is a measure of how capable a particular material or object is of storing an electrical charge. It is expressed as a ratio: the change in electrical charge in response to a difference in electrical potential. Capacitance can refer to either **self-capacitance**, where the difference in electrical potential is measured between the object in question and the ground, or **mutual capacitance**, where the difference in potential is measured between two objects or components. Self-capacitance is measured by how much electrical charge it takes to increase the electrical potential of the component by one volt (or other unit of measurement).

Impedance

Reactance and resistance are similar in that they both measure a force in opposition to an electrical current. Combining the effects of the two is **impedance**, which extends resistance into alternating current by giving it phase in addition to magnitude. Impedance can be complex to calculate, but it's useful for determining the best-quality signal you can output. The **maximum power theorem** states that to transfer the most power from a source to an output—such as from your microphone to your antenna—the impedance at the source should match the impedance at the output. Essentially, if you can keep your whole radio station operating at the same impedance, you will have the best-quality signal you can output.

Subelement G5 – Electrical Principles

Impedance Transformation

This maximum power theorem, and the idea of keeping impedance equal at both the input and output for maximum power strength, leads to a concept known as **impedance transformation**. Impedance transformation is the act of maintaining equal impedance across the entire circuit, which minimizes noise within the circuit and improves overall signal quality of outgoing signals. To make this easier to accomplish, many stations use a specific transformer network: a network of various components that allow impedance to be variably controlled. Essentially, it's a middleman in the electrical network that's used to adjust the circuit's impedance rather than trying to optimize it on every individual component of the entire circuit. Keep in mind that even when impedance is equal at both the input and output, you will need twice the actual desired power output. Maximized power efficiency is only fifty percent, since an equal amount of power will be both delivered to the load and dissipated.

Resonance

Imagine an object is swinging from a pendulum, and you want to maintain this swinging with the minimum amount of extra force possible. A regular, slight, momentum-reinforcing push at the right moment will keep the pendulum going with minimal expended effort. This is the concept of **resonance**, and it applies to oscillating electrical frequencies as well.

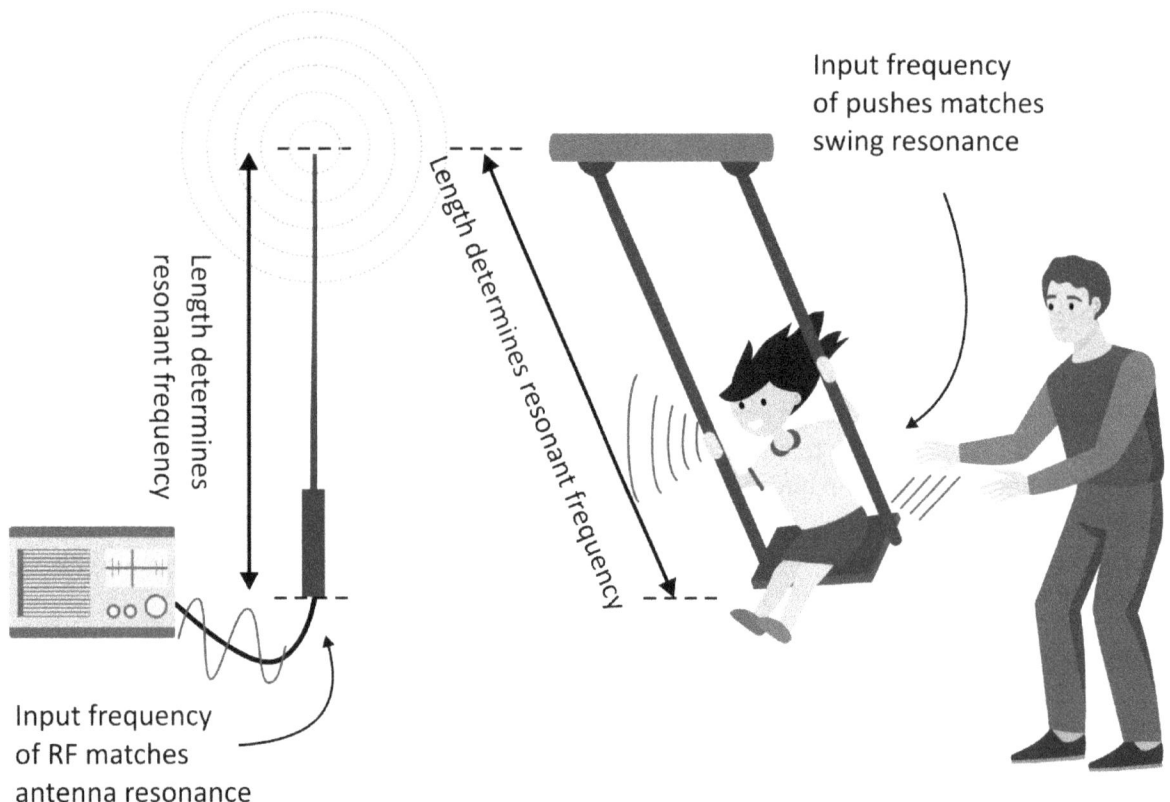

The length of a radio antenna determines the period of oscillation, and the radio frequency from the transmitter determines the "timing" of the electrical "pushes." If there is too much of a mismatch between the oscillation period on the antenna and the radio frequency, it can lead to very inefficient power usage. We can't always change the radio frequency to optimize this, since we may need to be

Subelement G5 – Electrical Principles

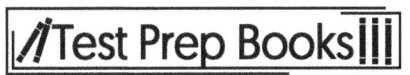

broadcasting on a specific frequency. The only other solution is to optimize the length of the antenna to the intended frequency. In short, an antenna length that is optimal for the frequencies you plan to broadcast on helps maximize power efficiency. Don't worry about needing to own multiple antennas, though. While that is an option for more hardcore amateurs, it's common to have a single antenna that's able to cover a majority of, if not all of, a particular Amateur Radio Service band.

G5B

The Decibel

You may have heard of decibels before, usually in the context of loud noises or music. The **decibel (dB)** is a unit of measurement that may be used to express a variety of different things but is mostly used in electronics and acoustics. Decibels don't have a unit themselves, but instead measure the difference between two quantities of the same type of unit, such as watts for voltage. If the second quantity is larger than the first, decibels are positive; if the second is smaller than the first, decibels are negative. For example, amplifying an audio signal may apply a gain of 6 dB.

Decibels can be confusing to understand because they operate on multiple scaling factors. They are expressed as a logarithm in base 10, but changes in amplitude are additionally scaled down by a factor of two. The following table shows this in more detail:

dB	Power ratio	Amplitude ratio
0	1	1
1	1.259	1.122
3	1.995	1.413
6	3.981	1.995
10	10	3.162
20	100	10
30	1,000	31.62
40	10,000	100

Decibels mostly come up in amateur radio when amplifying audio through gain or when measuring a signal-to-noise ratio, and they simplify the measurements down into scalable numbers instead of using complex notations. In most cases, you'll be operating on a decibel range between –10 and 10, so focus on memorizing a few key decibel ratios in that range.

Subelement G5 – Electrical Principles

Current and Voltage Dividers

Voltage divider circuits (also sometimes called series circuits) use multiple resistors in a single circuit and divide the voltage across all the resistors in the circuit. As an example of how this works, look at the diagram below that shows a simple series circuit with two resistors.

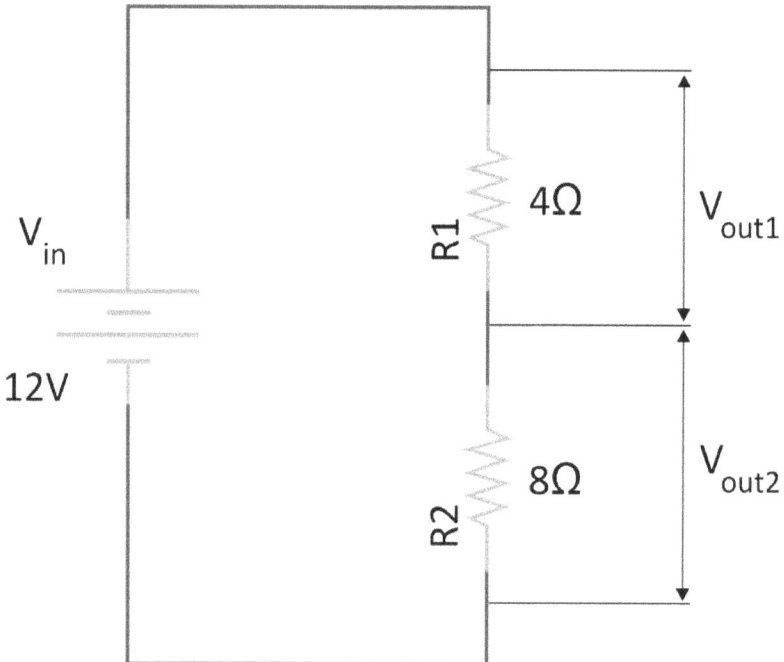

Since both resistors are part of the same circuit, the voltage is divided across both when finding the voltage passing through each one. Using the following equation, where R_x is the specific resistor, you're looking at and R_{total} is the combined total resistance in the circuit:

$$V_{out} = V_{in} \times \frac{R_x}{R_{total}}$$

In the above example, V_{out1} is 4V and V_{out2} is 8V. Thus, the input of 12V has been divided across both resistors—a voltage divider circuit. Voltage divider circuits are used in devices like potentiometers to create variable amounts of resistance in a circuit.

Subelement G5 – Electrical Principles

Current divider circuits (also sometimes called parallel circuits) are a similar concept, but they separate the resistors onto parallel lanes to divide current evenly between them. As an example of how this works, look at the diagram below that shows a simple parallel circuit with two resistors.

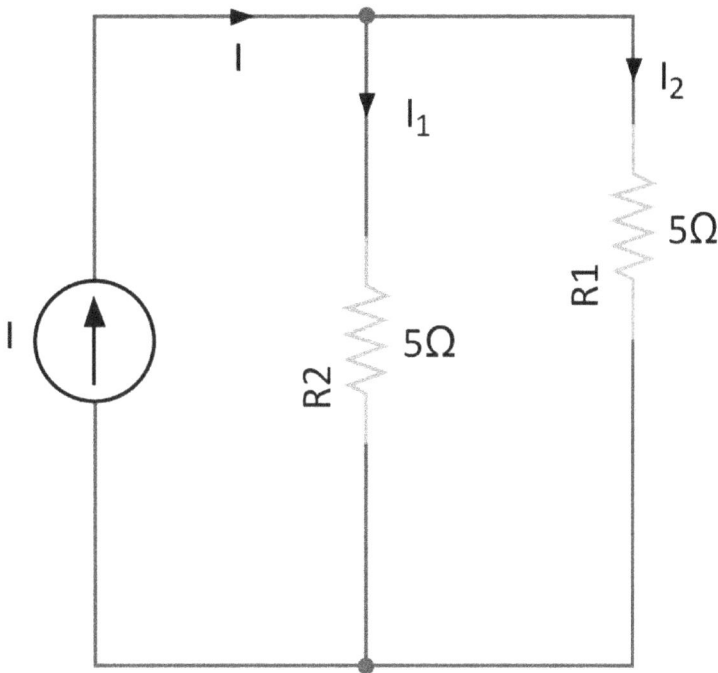

Both resistors are on the same circuit, but the current has two different paths to take. The current on a given path can be calculated using the following equation, where n is the specific path and resistor, and R_{eq} is the equivalent resistance of all parallel resistors, calculated using the second equation:

$$I_n = I_{in} \times \frac{R_{eq}}{R_n}$$

$$R_{eq} = \frac{1}{\left(\frac{1}{R_1}\right) + \left(\frac{1}{R_2}\right)}$$

In the above example, R_{eq} is 2.5 ohms, and the final current is split perfectly evenly between both paths—5 amperes on each. Current divider circuits can be used to help simplify resistor predictions, and many circuits are either a voltage divider, current divider, or both.

Electrical Power Calculations

When calculating the power used by a circuit, the resistance or impedance may be referred to as the **load**. The load generally refers to the resistance or impedance of an entire circuit. From there, it's important to keep two key electrical principles in mind: **Ohm's Law**, and the **Power Law**.

Ohm's Law: $V = I \times R$ where V is voltage, I is current, and R is resistance.

Power Law: $P = V \times I$ where P is power in watts, V is voltage, and I is current.

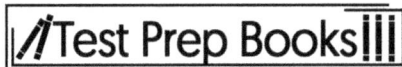

Subelement G5 – Electrical Principles

Keep in mind that these are variables that can be moved around the equation; for example, $I = \frac{V}{R}$ is an equally correct interpretation of Ohm's Law.

Let's say you want to calculate the power usage of a circuit, but you are only provided with the voltage and resistance: 300V and 600 ohms. By changing Ohm's Law into a variant that solves for current, you can substitute it in place of current within the Power Law to calculate the power.

$$P = V \times I = V \times \frac{V}{R} = 300 \times \frac{300}{600} = 200 \times \frac{1}{2} = 100 \; watts$$

Since voltage and current are shared in both Ohm's Law and the Power Law, keep in mind that you can substitute variations of them into each other, and you can solve many power calculations easily.

Sine Wave Root-Mean-Square (RMS) Values

Power calculations in alternating current (AC) are more complicated since this type of current is an alternating waveform, and therefore many of its characteristics are in constant fluctuation. Because of this, the **Root-Mean-Square** method is used to generate an effective value from values over time that is equivalent to a similar calculation for direct current at a single moment in time. Three mathematical operations are calculated on an AC waveform to determine its RMS value:

- First, the square of the waveform is determined, usually using a sine wave.
- Next, the results from the previous calculation are averaged over time.
- Finally, the square root of the results from the second step's calculation is found.

RMS values are used for alternating currents to try to equate them to a similar direct current value. Keep in mind that the RMS value is for an average comparison; the actual values of an AC's peaks are likely to be much higher and lower. The sine wave of an AC's waveform is the most used, so the RMS value is usually about 0.707 times the peak value of the waveform. If a device using AC claims to be a 200 volt circuit, the actual peak is roughly 283 volts.

Subelement G5 – Electrical Principles

PEP Calculations

PEP stands for **Peak Envelope Power** and refers to the average power in one cycle at the peaks of the waveform. It's important to know PEP, as this will determine the power used to swing between the peaks of an alternating current waveform at their strongest values. PEP is calculated with the following formula, and visualized with the following diagram:

$$PEP = \frac{(PEV \times 0.707)^2}{R}$$

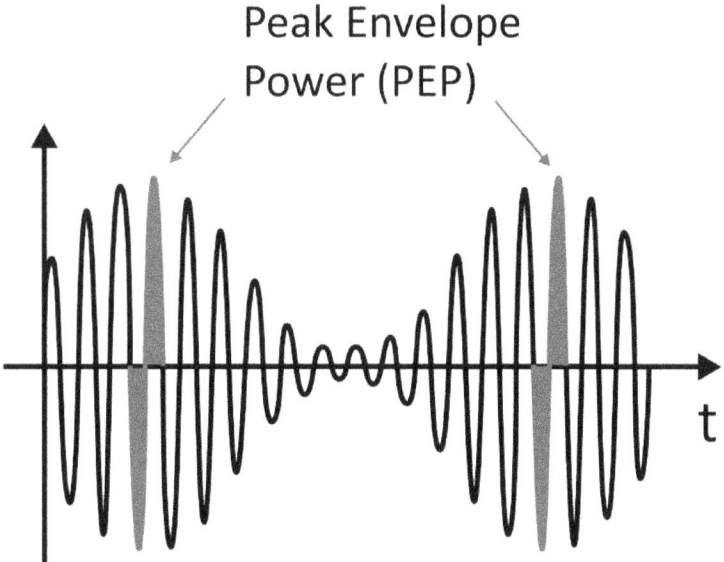

R is the resistance in ohms. PEV is the **Peak Envelope Voltage**, which can be measured by finding the amplitude of the waveform at its peak. That value is then multiplied by 0.707—a value you may remember from RMS sine wave calculations—to find the average voltage over that period. This average will be lower because we are already using the peak voltage. This results in a formula that is a variation of the Power Law, where current is replaced by voltage divided by resistance.

For example, if you know a circuits PEV is 200 volts and its resistance is 80 ohms, then:

$$PEP = \frac{(200 \times 0.707)^2}{80} = \frac{(141.4)^2}{80} = \frac{19993.96}{80} = 249.92$$

The final Peak Envelope Power of this waveform is roughly 250 watts.

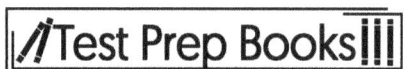

Subelement G5 – Electrical Principles

G5C

Resistors, Capacitors, and Inductors in Series and Parallel

In ham radio circuits, resistors, capacitors, and inductors are passive electronic components used to control the flow of current and voltage in a circuit and to filter out unwanted signals.

A **resistor** is an electronic component that resists the flow of current in a circuit. It is used to limit the amount of current flowing through a particular part of the circuit. In a series circuit, resistors are connected one after another, and the circuit's total resistance is the sum of the individual resistances. In a parallel circuit, resistors are connected side by side, and the total resistance is calculated using the reciprocal sum of the individual resistances.

A **capacitor** stores energy between two conductive plates. The insulating material separating the two plates is called the dielectric. Capacitors are used in circuits to store and release energy quickly. In a series circuit, capacitors are connected end-to-end, and the total capacitance is calculated using the reciprocal of the sum of the individual capacitances. In a parallel circuit, capacitors are connected side by side, and the total capacitance is the sum of individual capacitances.

An **inductor** is designed to store energy in a magnetic field with a coil of wire. Inductors are used in circuits to filter out unwanted frequencies and to store and release energy over a longer period. In a series circuit, inductors are connected end-to-end, and the total inductance is the sum of the individual inductances. In a parallel circuit, inductors are connected side by side, and the total inductance is calculated using the reciprocal sum of the individual inductances.

Transformers

In the world of ham radio, transformers play a vital role in helping to match the impedance (the opposition to an alternating current) between a radio transmitter and an antenna. A **transformer** is designed to transfer energy between two circuits using electromagnetic induction. As it pertains to ham radio, transformers are used to convert the impedance of the transmitter's output to match the impedance of the antenna.

Impedance, measured in ohms, is a complex quantity that has both a magnitude and a phase angle. Many factors can affect the impedance of a circuit, including its resistance, inductance, and capacitance.

When the impedance of the transmitter output does not match the impedance of the antenna, a mismatch occurs that can result in power loss and reduced efficiency. This is generally where transformers come in. A transformer can match the impedance of the transmitter output to the impedance of the antenna, which allows for maximum power transfer and efficient operation.

Transformers consist of two or more coils of wire wrapped around a core made of magnetic material. When an alternating current flows through the primary coil, it creates a magnetic field that induces a current in the secondary coil. The ratio of the number of turns of wire in the primary coil to the number of turns in the secondary coil determines the impedance transformation ratio.

Subelement G5 – Electrical Principles

There are multiple types of transformers used in ham radio, each with its own characteristics and applications. The most common types are below:

- **Baluns** - A balun is used to convert between a balanced (two-wire) and an unbalanced (one-wire) signal. Baluns are commonly used in antenna systems to convert the unbalanced signal from a coaxial cable to a balanced signal that is used by many antennas.

- **Voltage transformers** - Voltage transformers are used to step up or step down the voltage of an AC signal. They are commonly used in power supplies and amplifiers to provide the correct voltage levels for the circuit.

- **Audio transformers** - Audio transformers are used to match the impedance of an audio signal to the input impedance of an amplifier. They are commonly used in audio equipment such as microphones, preamps, and mixers.

Subelement G5 - Questions

G5A

1. What happens when inductive and capacitive reactance are equal in a series LC circuit?
    A. Resonance causes impedance to be very high
    B. Impedance is equal to the geometric mean of the inductance and capacitance
    C. Resonance causes impedance to be very low
    D. Impedance is equal to the arithmetic mean of the inductance and capacitance

2. What is reactance?
    A. Opposition to the flow of direct current caused by resistance
    B. Opposition to the flow of alternating current caused by capacitance or inductance
    C. Reinforcement of the flow of direct current caused by resistance
    D. Reinforcement of the flow of alternating current caused by capacitance or inductance

3. Which of the following is opposition to the flow of alternating current in an inductor?
    A. Conductance
    B. Reluctance
    C. Admittance
    D. Reactance

4. Which of the following is opposition to the flow of alternating current in a capacitor?
    A. Conductance
    B. Reluctance
    C. Reactance
    D. Admittance

5. How does an inductor react to AC?
    A. As the frequency of the applied AC increases, the reactance decreases
    B. As the amplitude of the applied AC increases, the reactance increases
    C. As the amplitude of the applied AC increases, the reactance decreases
    D. As the frequency of the applied AC increases, the reactance increases

6. How does a capacitor react to AC?
    A. As the frequency of the applied AC increases, the reactance decreases
    B. As the frequency of the applied AC increases, the reactance increases
    C. As the amplitude of the applied AC increases, the reactance increases
    D. As the amplitude of the applied AC increases, the reactance decreases

7. What is the term for the inverse of impedance?
    A. Conductance
    B. Susceptance
    C. Reluctance
    D. Admittance

Subelement G5 – Electrical Principles

8. What is impedance?
    A. The ratio of current to voltage
    B. The product of current and voltage
    C. The ratio of voltage to current
    D. The product of current and reactance

9. What unit is used to measure reactance?
    A. Farad
    B. Ohm
    C. Ampere
    D. Siemens

10. Which of the following devices can be used for impedance matching at radio frequencies?
    A. A transformer
    B. A Pi-network
    C. A length of transmission line
    D. All these choices are correct

11. What letter is used to represent reactance?
    A. Z
    B. X
    C. B
    D. Y

12. What occurs in an LC circuit at resonance?
    A. Current and voltage are equal
    B. Resistance is cancelled
    C. The circuit radiates all its energy in the form of radio waves
    D. Inductive reactance and capacitive reactance cancel

G5B

1. What dB change represents a factor of two increase or decrease in power?
    A. Approximately 2 dB
    B. Approximately 3 dB
    C. Approximately 6 dB
    D. Approximately 9 dB

2. How does the total current relate to the individual currents in a circuit of parallel resistors?
    A. It equals the average of the branch currents
    B. It decreases as more parallel branches are added to the circuit
    C. It equals the sum of the currents through each branch
    D. It is the sum of the reciprocal of each individual voltage drop

3. How many watts of electrical power are consumed if 400 VDC is supplied to an 800-ohm load?
    A. 0.5 watts
    B. 200 watts
    C. 400 watts
    D. 3200 watts

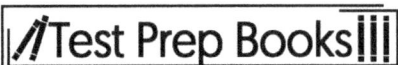

Subelement G5 – Electrical Principles

4. How many watts of electrical power are consumed by a 12 VDC light bulb that draws 0.2 amperes?
   A. 2.4 watts
   B. 24 watts
   C. 6 watts
   D. 60 watts

5. How many watts are consumed when a current of 7.0 milliamperes flows through a 1,250-ohm resistance?
   A. Approximately 61 milliwatts
   B. Approximately 61 watts
   C. Approximately 11 milliwatts
   D. Approximately 11 watts

6. What is the PEP produced by 200 volts peak-to-peak across a 50-ohm dummy load?
   A. 1.4 watts
   B. 100 watts
   C. 353.5 watts
   D. 400 watts

7. What value of an AC signal produces the same power dissipation in a resistor as a DC voltage of the same value?
   A. The peak-to-peak value
   B. The peak value
   C. The RMS value
   D. The reciprocal of the RMS value

8. What is the peak-to-peak voltage of a sine wave with an RMS voltage of 120 volts?
   A. 84.8 volts
   B. 169.7 volts
   C. 240.0 volts
   D. 339.4 volts

9. What is the RMS voltage of a sine wave with a value of 17 volts peak?
   A. 8.5 volts
   B. 12 volts
   C. 24 volts
   D. 34 volts

10. What percentage of power loss is equivalent to a loss of 1 dB?
    A. 10.9 percent
    B. 12.2 percent
    C. 20.6 percent
    D. 25.9 percent

11. What is the ratio of PEP to average power for an unmodulated carrier?
    A. 0.707
    B. 1.00
    C. 1.414
    D. 2.00

12. What is the RMS voltage across a 50-ohm dummy load dissipating 1200 watts?
    A. 173 volts
    B. 245 volts
    C. 346 volts
    D. 692 volts

13. What is the output PEP of an unmodulated carrier if the average power is 1060 watts?
    A. 530 watts
    B. 1060 watts
    C. 1500 watts
    D. 2120 watts

14. What is the output PEP of 500 volts peak-to-peak across a 50-ohm load?
    A. 8.75 watts
    B. 625 watts
    C. 2500 watts
    D. 5000 watts

G5C

1. What causes a voltage to appear across the secondary winding of a transformer when an AC voltage source is connected across its primary winding?
    A. Capacitive coupling
    B. Displacement current coupling
    C. Mutual inductance
    D. Mutual capacitance

2. What is the output voltage if an input signal is applied to the secondary winding of a 4:1 voltage step-down transformer instead of the primary winding?
    A. The input voltage is multiplied by 4
    B. The input voltage is divided by 4
    C. Additional resistance must be added in series with the primary to prevent overload
    D. Additional resistance must be added in parallel with the secondary to prevent overload

3. What is the total resistance of a 10-, a 20-, and a 50-ohm resistor connected in parallel?
    A. 5.9 ohms
    B. 0.17 ohms
    C. 17 ohms
    D. 80 ohms

4. What is the approximate total resistance of a 100- and a 200-ohm resistor in parallel?
    A. 300 ohms
    B. 150 ohms
    C. 75 ohms
    D. 67 ohms

5. Why is the primary winding wire of a voltage step-up transformer usually a larger size than that of the secondary winding?
    A. To improve the coupling between the primary and secondary
    B. To accommodate the higher current of the primary
    C. To prevent parasitic oscillations due to resistive losses in the primary
    D. To ensure that the volume of the primary winding is equal to the volume of the secondary winding

6. What is the voltage output of a transformer with a 500-turn primary and a 1500-turn secondary when 120 VAC is applied to the primary?
    A. 360 volts
    B. 120 volts
    C. 40 volts
    D. 25.5 volts

7. What transformer turns ratio matches an antenna's 600-ohm feed point impedance to a 50-ohm coaxial cable?
    A. 3.5 to 1
    B. 12 to 1
    C. 24 to 1
    D. 144 to 1

8. What is the equivalent capacitance of two 5.0-nanofarad capacitors and one 750-picofarad capacitor connected in parallel?
    A. 576.9 nanofarads
    B. 1,733 picofarads
    C. 3,583 picofarads
    D. 10.750 nanofarads

9. What is the capacitance of three 100-microfarad capacitors connected in series?
    A. 0.33 microfarads
    B. 3.0 microfarads
    C. 33.3 microfarads
    D. 300 microfarads

10. What is the inductance of three 10-millihenry inductors connected in parallel?
    A. 0.30 henries
    B. 3.3 henries
    C. 3.3 millihenries
    D. 30 millihenries

11. What is the inductance of a circuit with a 20-millihenry inductor connected in series with a 50-millihenry inductor?
    A. 7 millihenries
    B. 14.3 millihenries
    C. 70 millihenries
    D. 1,000 millihenries

Subelement G5 – Electrical Principles

12. What is the capacitance of a 20-microfarad capacitor connected in series with a 50-microfarad capacitor?
    A. 0.07 microfarads
    B. 14.3 microfarads
    C. 70 microfarads
    D. 1,000 microfarads

13. Which of the following components should be added to a capacitor to increase the capacitance?
    A. An inductor in series
    B. An inductor in parallel
    C. A capacitor in parallel
    D. A capacitor in series

14. Which of the following components should be added to an inductor to increase the inductance?
    A. A capacitor in series
    B. A capacitor in parallel
    C. An inductor in parallel
    D. An inductor in series

Subelement G5 – Answer Key

G5A

1. C	7. D
2. B	8. C
3. D	9. B
4. C	10. D
5. D	11. B
6. A	12. D

G5B

1. B	8. D
2. C	9. B
3. B	10. C
4. A	11. B
5. A	12. B
6. B	13. B
7. C	14. B

G5C

1. C	8. D
2. A	9. C
3. A	10. C
4. D	11. C
5. B	12. B
6. A	13. C
7. A	14. D

Subelement G6 – Circuit Components

G6A

Resistors

In ham radio systems, a **resistor** is a passive two-terminal component that resists the flow of a circuit's electric current. Resistors are designed to drop the voltage in a circuit. They are commonly used in ham radio circuits for three primary purposes: providing biasing for active components, limiting the amount of current flowing through a circuit, and adjusting the impedance of a circuit. These purposes are explained in further detail below:

Resistors in ham radio circuits are critical for biasing active components of the circuit, such as transistors and operational amplifiers. A resistor is used to set the base voltage of a transistor to a degree that ensures proper operation. The value of the resistor can be adjusted to achieve the desired bias voltage, which determines the flow of current through the transistor. The same concept applies to operational amplifiers, where a resistor is used to set the input bias current.

The other essential application of resistors in ham radio circuits is in limiting the current flow through a circuit. Resistors are used as current-limiting components to prevent the overload of other electronic components in the circuit. In ham radio circuits, this is crucial for preventing damage to sensitive components and keeping the entire ham radio in working order.

Resistors also play a crucial role in the impedance matching of ham radio circuits. Impedance matching is a process of matching the impedance of a circuit to the source or load impedance. A resistor adjusts the impedance of a circuit to match the required impedance and ensures maximum power transfer.

Capacitors

A **capacitor** stores electrical energy in an electric field. The amount of charge that a capacitor can store is determined by its capacitance, which is measured in Farads.

Ham radio capacitors, like many other ham radio components, have multiple uses. A common use drawn directly from its primary function is energy storage. Capacitors create an electric field between two conductive plates that are separated by a non-conductive material known as the dielectric. When a voltage is applied to the capacitor, electrons accumulate on one plate, creating a negative charge, while the other plate becomes positively charged due to the lack of electrons. In this way, capacitors can store electrical energy and release it quickly when needed. This can be useful in applications where a quick burst of energy is needed, such as in a radio transmitter. By storing energy in a capacitor and releasing it quickly, a transmitter can generate a high-power signal for short periods of time.

Capacitors are also used in tuning circuits to adjust the resonant frequency of a circuit. When the capacitance is changed, the frequency of the circuit can be adjusted to match the desired frequency of operation. Frequency control is critical for the proper operation of ham radios and any other type of radio transmitter or receiver.

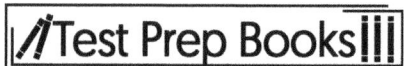

Subelement G6 – Circuit Components

Additionally, capacitors are used in filtering circuits, where they help to remove unwanted signals and strip unwanted noise from retained signals. For example, in a radio receiver, capacitors can be used to block high-frequency signals and allow only the desired frequency to pass through. This helps improve the signal-to-noise ratio and reduce interference, thereby increasing the ham radio's overall clarity.

Inductors

Inductors, also known as coils or chokes, are commonly used in radio frequency circuits.

One of the primary applications of inductors in ham radio systems is in filters. Filters are circuits designed to pass certain frequencies while blocking others. A resonant circuit is a type of filter that is created when an inductor and a capacitor are combined. For example, a high-pass filter can be created by placing an inductor in series with a capacitor. This combination allows high frequencies to pass while blocking low frequencies.

Another application of inductors in ham radio systems is in impedance-matching circuits. Impedance matching is crucial in radio systems because it ensures that maximum power is transferred from the transmitter to the antenna. Inductors are used in these circuits to match the impedance of the transmitter to the impedance of the antenna. This is accomplished by adjusting the number of turns or the core material of the inductor, which can tune the inductor to a specific frequency.

Inductors are also used in oscillators, circuits that produce an alternating current (AC) signal at a specific frequency. In oscillators, both the inductor and a capacitor determine the frequency of the signal. The signal's frequency can be adjusted by varying the value of the inductor or capacitor. This is important in ham radio systems because different frequencies are used for different types and channels of communication.

Rectifiers

Rectifiers are widely used in ham radio systems for converting alternating current (AC) to direct current (DC). They are often used in power supply circuits to provide the necessary DC voltage for powering radio equipment.

Several types of rectifiers can be used in ham radio systems, the most common of which are **diode rectifiers**. They consist of one or more diodes that are connected in series with the load. When AC voltage is applied to the circuit, the diode or diodes conduct only during the positive half-cycle, allowing current to flow through the load in one direction. During the negative half-cycle, the diode or diodes are reverse-biased and prevent current from flowing.

Bridge rectifiers, on the other hand, consist of four diodes that are arranged in a bridge configuration. They allow current to flow through the load in one direction during both the positive and negative half-cycles of the AC voltage. Bridge rectifiers are more efficient than diode rectifiers because they use both halves of the AC cycle.

Vacuum tube rectifiers are not as common in modern ham radio systems, but they were widely used in the past. They consist of a vacuum tube that functions as a rectifier. When the tube is heated, electrons are emitted from the cathode and flow toward the anode. When AC voltage is applied to the circuit, the electrons flow toward the anode during the positive half-cycle, allowing current to flow through the load in one direction.

Subelement G6 – Circuit Components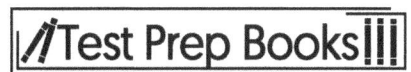

Rectifiers are also used in signal detection circuits, such as in envelope detectors, which are used for demodulating amplitude-modulated (AM) signals. In envelope detectors, the rectifier converts the modulated RF signal to a varying DC voltage that represents the audio signal.

Solid-State Diodes and Transistors

Solid-state diodes and transistors offer advantages over vacuum tube-based devices, such as compact size, improved reliability, and lower power consumption. The uses of these devices are discussed below:

Solid-state diodes are semiconductor devices that allow current to flow in one direction only, providing rectification of alternating current (AC) to direct current (DC). In ham radio systems, diodes are used in power supplies for rectifying AC from the mains or a transformer to DC voltage required for powering various equipment, including amplifiers and transceivers. Diodes are also used in envelope detectors for demodulating amplitude-modulated (AM) signals, where the rectification process recovers the amplitude-modulated information from the carrier signal.

Transistors, on the other hand, are semiconductor devices that act as amplifiers and switches in ham radio systems. The most common types of transistors used in ham radio systems are bipolar junction transistors (BJTs) and field-effect transistors (FETs). BJTs have three regions: the emitter, the base, and the collector. In ham radio systems, they are used as amplifiers in low-level RF and audio circuits, as well as in power amplifiers for higher-power applications. FETs have a gate, a source, and a drain, and are used in radio frequency (RF) and microwave circuits as amplifiers, oscillators, and mixers.

In addition to their use in amplification, transistors can be used as switches in ham radio systems. The transistor can be turned on and off rapidly using a control signal, which allows it to act as a switch in RF and digital circuits. Transistors can also be used in oscillator circuits, where they are able to generate a continuous waveform at a specific frequency. This is crucial for transmitting and receiving signals at specific frequencies in ham radio systems.

Furthermore, transistors can be used in frequency modulation (FM) circuits, where the voltage applied to the transistor's base determines the frequency of the output signal. In FM circuits, the transistor modulates a carrier wave with an audio signal, allowing for the transmission of high-quality audio signals over long distances.

Vacuum Tubes

Vacuum tubes, also known as electron tubes, were once the primary electronic components used in electronic equipment before the turn to solid-state technology. These devices consist of a sealed glass or metal container containing a vacuum with various electrodes and elements inside. They are used to control the flow of electrons. Vacuum tubes played a particularly significant role in the early days of ham radio.

Among the most common uses of vacuum tubes in ham radio systems is in the amplification of signals. In a typical ham radio system, a small electrical signal is generated by a microphone or other input device. The signal is then sent to an amplifier. The amplifier increases the strength of the signal, which allows it to be transmitted over greater distances. Vacuum tubes are well-suited for this task because they can handle high power levels without breaking down, and they are relatively easy to control.

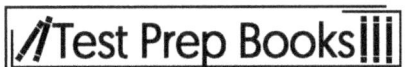

Subelement G6 – Circuit Components

Vacuum tubes are also useful in ham radio systems for signal modulation. **Modulation** is the process of varying the amplitude, frequency, or phase of a carrier wave to transmit information. In ham radio, modulation is typically used to transmit voice or data. Vacuum tubes can be used as modulators because they can vary the current or voltage of a signal in a precise and controlled manner.

Vacuum tubes are also used as rectifiers in ham radio systems, although this is uncommon in modern systems. As mentioned under G6A: Rectifiers, a rectifier converts alternating current into direct current. In ham radio, rectifiers are used to power the various components of the system. The high voltage capacity of vacuum tube rectifiers makes them ideal for high-power applications.

In addition, vacuum tubes may be used as oscillators in ham radio systems. As explained in G6A: Inductors, an oscillator is a device that generates a continuous signal at a specific frequency. Vacuum tube oscillators are popular because they can generate high-frequency signals with good stability and low noise.

Batteries

Batteries are an essential component of ham radio systems, as they provide portable and reliable power to radios and associated equipment. These power sources come in a variety of chemistries, sizes, and voltages, each with their own benefits and drawbacks.

Among the most popular types of batteries for ham radio systems is the lead-acid battery. These batteries are cost-effective and durable, which makes them an excellent choice for powering base stations and backup power systems. They come in sealed or flooded varieties. Sealed batteries are the preferred option for indoor use due to their lower maintenance requirements. Flooded lead-acid batteries require more maintenance but have a longer lifespan and are better suited for outdoor use.

Another type of battery commonly used in ham radio systems is the lithium-ion battery. These batteries are lightweight and have a high energy density, making them ideal for portable operations. While they are highly efficient and have a long lifespan, they are more expensive than lead-acid batteries.

Other types of batteries used in ham radio systems include nickel-cadmium (NiCad) and nickel-metal hydride (NiMH) batteries. NiCad batteries are reliable and have a long lifespan, but they are less efficient than lithium-ion batteries and have a higher self-discharge rate. NiMH batteries are like NiCad batteries but have a higher energy density and lower self-discharge rate.

When selecting a battery for a ham radio system, consider factors such as the power requirements of the radio and other equipment, the duration of use, and the portability of the system. It is also important to select a battery with the appropriate voltage and capacity to reliably operate the system.

In addition to powering radios and associated equipment, batteries can also power emergency communications systems. Ham radio operators often use batteries as a backup power source in case of a power outage or other emergency, which ensures they can continue to communicate even when the grid is down.

Subelement G6 – Circuit Components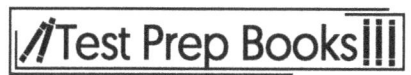

G6B

Analog and Digital Integrated Circuits (ICs)

Integrated circuits (ICs) are electronic components that contain multiple transistors, resistors, and other components on a single chip. ICs can be classified into two main categories: analog and digital.

Analog ICs are designed to work with continuously varying signals, such as those found in audio or radio frequency (RF) applications. These ICs are used in ham radio systems for a variety of purposes, including amplification, filtering, and modulation. For example, an analog IC may be used in a preamplifier circuit to boost the weak signal from an antenna before it is sent to the radio's main amplifier. Analog filters can reduce unwanted signals or noise in the received signal, while analog modulators can convert the audio signal from a microphone into a modulated RF signal.

Digital ICs are designed to work with discrete binary signals, such as those used in digital signal processing (DSP) applications. These ICs are used in ham radio systems for tasks such as frequency synthesis, data decoding, and digital signal processing. For example, a digital frequency synthesizer IC can be used to generate stable and accurate RF signals for testing or calibration purposes.

A combination of analog and digital ICs may be used to achieve the desired functionality. For example, a radio may use an analog preamplifier to boost the signal from an antenna, followed by a digital downconverter to convert the RF signal to a digital intermediate frequency (IF) signal for further processing. The digital IF signal may then be processed by a digital signal processor to extract the audio signal, which can be further amplified and filtered by analog ICs before being sent to the radio's speaker.

Microwave ICs (MMICs)

Microwave ICs (MMICs) are a type of integrated circuit designed to operate at microwave frequencies, typically ranging from 1 GHz to 100 GHz. MMICs are used in ham radio systems for such purposes as amplification, filtering, mixing, and oscillation.

MMICs are made using specialized fabrication processes that allow for the creation of the very small and precise components, such as transistors and capacitors, needed to operate at these high frequencies. MMICs are also designed with low noise and high linearity characteristics, making them ideal for use in radio frequency (RF) systems.

In ham radio systems, MMICs are used to provide high-gain amplification for low-power signals, as well as for frequency conversion and filtering. For example, an MMIC may be used in a preamplifier circuit to boost the signal from an antenna before it is sent to the radio's main amplifier. MMICs can also be used in mixers to convert the frequency of the RF signal to a lower intermediate frequency (IF) signal for further processing.

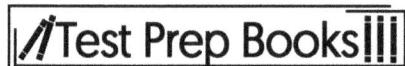

Display Devices

Display devices are electronic components used to display information in ham radio systems. The type of display device used depends on the specific application and the desired level of functionality.

A common type of display device used in ham radio systems is the **liquid crystal display (LCD)**. LCDs are relatively low power and can display a wide range of information, including frequency, mode, and signal strength. They are commonly used in handheld radios and base stations.

Another type of display device used in ham radio systems is the **light-emitting diode (LED)**. LEDs are typically used to display simple information, such as power status or mode selection. They are low power and can be easily read in bright sunlight, which makes them a good choice for portable radios.

In some cases, more advanced display devices may be used in ham radio systems, such as touchscreen displays or **organic light-emitting diode (OLED)** displays. These displays provide more advanced functionality, such as the ability to display graphs or maps, and may be used in more advanced radios or test equipment.

RF Connectors

Radio frequency (RF) connectors allow for the connection of various radio components and antennas. RF connectors are designed to transmit RF signals with minimal signal loss and interference. They come in a variety of shapes and sizes to accommodate different applications. Some of the most common types of RF connectors in ham radio systems are as follows:

- **BNC connectors** are small, quick-connect RF connectors commonly used for low-power applications such as antennas and test equipment. They are easy to install and provide a secure connection.

- **N connectors** are threaded RF connectors commonly used for higher-power applications such as amplifiers and antennas. They provide a more secure connection than BNC connectors and can handle higher power levels.

- **SMA connectors** are small, threaded RF connectors commonly used for higher-frequency applications such as handheld radios and antennas. They are commonly used in portable or mobile applications.

- **UHF connectors** are threaded RF connectors commonly used for low-frequency applications such as VHF and UHF antennas. They are easy to install and provide a secure connection but are not recommended for high-power applications.

The choice of RF connector will depend on the specific application and frequency range of the radio. It's important to use the correct connector for each application to ensure optimal performance and minimize signal loss.

Ferrite Cores

Ferrite cores are magnetic cores made from a ceramic compound of iron oxide and other metal oxides. They are commonly used in ham radio systems to provide inductance and suppress **electromagnetic interference (EMI).**

Ferrite cores can be used to make inductors for filters, impedance-matching networks, and other RF circuits. The high permeability of ferrite material allows for a compact and efficient inductor design. This efficiency is especially important in portable and mobile radio applications where space is at a premium.

In addition to providing inductance, ferrite cores can be used to suppress EMI by absorbing or redirecting electromagnetic energy. Ferrite cores are often used in **RF chokes**, which can block unwanted RF signals from entering or leaving a circuit. Ferrite beads are another common use of ferrite cores in ham radio systems. These small cylindrical beads are threaded onto a wire or cable and act as a high-frequency filter, blocking EMI from entering or leaving the cable.

# Subelement G6 - Questions

G6A

1. What is the minimum allowable discharge voltage for maximum life of a standard 12-volt lead-acid battery?
    A. 6 volts
    B. 8.5 volts
    C. 10.5 volts
    D. 12 volts

2. What is an advantage of batteries with low internal resistance?
    A. Long life
    B. High discharge current
    C. High voltage
    D. Rapid recharge

3. What is the approximate forward threshold voltage of a germanium diode?
    A. 0.1 volt
    B. 0.3 volts
    C. 0.7 volts
    D. 1.0 volts

4. Which of the following is characteristic of an electrolytic capacitor?
    A. Tight tolerance
    B. Much less leakage than any other type
    C. High capacitance for a given volume
    D. Inexpensive RF capacitor

5. What is the approximate forward threshold voltage of a silicon junction diode?
    A. 0.1 volt
    B. 0.3 volts
    C. 0.7 volts
    D. 1.0 volts

6. Why should wire-wound resistors not be used in RF circuits?
    A. The resistor's tolerance value would not be adequate
    B. The resistor's inductance could make circuit performance unpredictable
    C. The resistor could overheat
    D. The resistor's internal capacitance would detune the circuit

7. What are the operating points for a bipolar transistor used as a switch?
    A. Saturation and cutoff
    B. The active region (between cutoff and saturation)
    C. Peak and valley current points
    D. Enhancement and depletion modes

8. Which of the following is characteristic of low voltage ceramic capacitors?
   A. Tight tolerance
   B. High stability
   C. High capacitance for given volume
   D. Comparatively low cost

9. Which of the following describes MOSFET construction?
   A. The gate is formed by a back-biased junction
   B. The gate is separated from the channel by a thin insulating layer
   C. The source is separated from the drain by a thin insulating layer
   D. The source is formed by depositing metal on silicon

10. Which element of a vacuum tube regulates the flow of electrons between cathode and plate?
    A. Control grid
    B. Suppressor grid
    C. Screen grid
    D. Trigger electrode

11. What happens when an inductor is operated above its self-resonant frequency?
    A. Its reactance increases
    B. Harmonics are generated
    C. It becomes capacitive
    D. Catastrophic failure is likely

12. What is the primary purpose of a screen grid in a vacuum tube?
    A. To reduce grid-to-plate capacitance
    B. To increase efficiency
    C. To increase the control grid resistance
    D. To decrease plate resistance

G6B

1. What determines the performance of a ferrite core at different frequencies?
   A. Its conductivity
   B. Its thickness
   C. The composition, or "mix," of materials used
   D. The ratio of outer diameter to inner diameter

2. What is meant by the term MMIC?
   A. Multi-Mode Integrated Circuit
   B. Monolithic Microwave Integrated Circuit
   C. Metal Monolayer Integrated Circuit
   D. Mode Modulated Integrated Circuit

3. Which of the following is an advantage of CMOS integrated circuits compared to TTL integrated circuits?
    A. Low power consumption
    B. High power handling capability
    C. Better suited for RF amplification
    D. Better suited for power supply regulation

4. What is a typical upper frequency limit for low SWR operation of 50-ohm BNC connectors?
    A. 50 MHz
    B. 500 MHz
    C. 4 GHz
    D. 40 GHz

5. What is an advantage of using a ferrite core toroidal inductor?
    A. Large values of inductance may be obtained
    B. The magnetic properties of the core may be optimized for a specific range of frequencies
    C. Most of the magnetic field is contained in the core
    D. All these choices are correct

6. What kind of device is an integrated circuit operational amplifier?
    A. Digital
    B. MMIC
    C. Programmable Logic
    D. Analog

7. Which of the following describes a type N connector?
    A. A moisture-resistant RF connector useful to 10 GHz
    B. A small bayonet connector used for data circuits
    C. A low noise figure VHF connector
    D. A nickel plated version of the PL-259

8. How is an LED biased when emitting light?
    A. In the tunnel-effect region
    B. At the Zener voltage
    C. Reverse biased
    D. Forward biased

9. How does a liquid crystal display compare to an LED display?
    A. Higher contrast in high ambient lighting
    B. Wider dynamic range
    C. Higher power consumption
    D. Shorter lifetime

10. How does a ferrite bead or core reduce common-mode RF current on the shield of a coaxial cable?
    A. By creating an impedance in the current's path
    B. It converts common-mode current to differential mode current
    C. By creating an out-of-phase current to cancel the common-mode current
    D. Ferrites expel magnetic fields

Subelement G6 – Circuit Components

11. What is an SMA connector?
    A. A type-S to type-M adaptor
    B. A small threaded connector suitable for signals up to several GHz
    C. A connector designed for serial multiple access signals
    D. A type of push-on connector intended for high-voltage applications

12. Which of these connector types is commonly used for low frequency or dc signal connections to a transceiver?
    A. PL-259
    B. BNC
    C. RCA Phono
    D. Type N

Subelement G6 – Answer Key

G6A

1. C	7. A
2. B	8. D
3. B	9. B
4. C	10. A
5. C	11. C
6. B	12. A

G6B

1. C	7. A
2. B	8. D
3. A	9. A
4. C	10. A
5. D	11. B
6. D	12. C

Subelement G7 – Practical Circuits

G7A

Power Supplies

Power supplies are systems of various circuit components in ham radio systems that provide the necessary power to operate the various radios, amplifiers, and other equipment used in the hobby. The type of power supply used depends on the specific application, power requirements, and desired level of functionality.

Linear power supplies are among the more common ham radio system power supply types. **Linear power supplies** use a transformer to step down the AC voltage from a wall outlet to a lower DC voltage suitable for use in the radio or other equipment. They provide a stable low-noise output and are relatively simple to design and build.

The other primary type of power supply used in ham radio systems is the switching power supply. **Switching power supplies** use a high-frequency oscillator to convert the AC voltage to DC, and then use a series of switching circuits to regulate the output voltage. They are more efficient than linear power supplies and can be designed to be smaller and lighter, which makes them a good choice for portable and mobile radio applications.

In addition to these standard types of power supplies, ham radio operators may also use battery power supplies or solar power supplies. Battery power supplies provide a portable, off-the-grid power solution for portable or mobile radio applications, while solar power supplies use photovoltaic panels to convert sunlight into electrical power for use in radio or other equipment.

The choice of power supply depends on the specific requirements of the ham radio system. For example, a high-power linear amplifier may require a high-voltage, high-current linear power supply, while a pocket radio may require a small, lightweight switching power supply or battery pack.

Regardless of the specific type of power supply used, it is important to ensure that the power supply provides clean, stable power to the radio or other equipment. Radio frequency interference (RFI) can be a problem in poorly designed or implemented power supplies, leading to unwanted noise or signal distortion in the radio. Proper filtering and shielding can help to reduce the effects of RFI on the power supply and the radio.

Schematic Symbols

Schematic symbols are graphical representations of electronic components and devices used in ham radio systems. These symbols are standardized and provide a convenient way to represent complex circuits and systems in a compact, easy-to-read format. The use of standardized symbols ensures that ham radio operators and technicians can easily read and interpret schematics, regardless of the specific equipment or system being used.

On the next page is a comprehensive list of the many schematic symbols that may be used in a ham radio system.

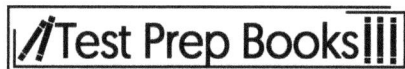

Electronic Schematic Symbols

Component	Symbol	Component	Symbol
Antenna		Relay	
Battery		Relay Contacts	
Bulb (indicator lamp)		Resistor	
Capacitor		Resistor (Tapped)	
Capacitor (Electrolytic)		Resistor (Variable, Potentiometer)	
Capacitor (Trimmer)		Silicon Controlled Rectifier (SCR)	
Capacitor (Variable)		Speaker	
Capacitor (Inductor)		Switch (SPST)	
Capacitor (Chassis)		Switch (Push Button)	
Capacitor (Wires)		Switch (Rotary)	
No-Connection (Wires)		Switch (SPDT)	
Crystal (Frequency)		Thermistor	
Diode		Transformer (Iron Core)	
Diode (Schottky)		Transformer (IF)	
Field Effect Transistor (FET) (N-Channel)		Transistor (NPN Bipolar)	
Field Effect Transistor (FET) (P-Channel)		Transistor (PNP Bipolar)	
Fuse		Vacuum Tube (Diode)	
Ground Connection		Vacuum Tube (Triode)	
Inductor		Vacuum Tube (Tetrode)	
Inductor (Iron Core)		Vacuum Tube (Pentode)	
Inductor (Variable)		Unijunction Transistor	
Light Emitting Diode (LED)		Varactor	
Microphone		Voltmeter	
Motor (Electric)		Zener Diode	
Phone Jack		Headphones	
Photo Cell		Coax or Shielded Cable	

G7B

Digital Circuits

What separates digital circuits from other electronic circuits is that they use digital signals to perform tasks such as logical operations and storing or processing data. They can control various aspects of ham radio systems and are used for a variety of purposes, as explained below.

Critically, digital circuits in ham radio systems use digital signal processing (DSP). DSP techniques allow ham radio operators to filter out unwanted noise and interference, enhance weak signals, and perform other signal-processing tasks. These techniques are implemented using specialized digital signal processors designed to perform complex mathematical calculations quickly and accurately.

Another use of digital circuits in ham radio systems is in modulation and demodulation. Digital modulation schemes, such as phase-shift keying (PSK) and frequency-shift keying (FSK), are used to transmit digital data over the airwaves. Digital demodulation techniques can recover digital data from the received signal. These techniques are often implemented with specialized digital signal processing circuits or integrated circuits.

Digital circuits are also used in frequency control circuits. Digital frequency synthesizers use digital signal processing techniques to generate precise, stable signals at a wide range of frequencies. These circuits are often used to generate local oscillator signals for use in mixers and other radio frequency circuits.

Data transmission is another area where digital circuits are commonly used in ham radio systems. Digital data modes, such as packet radio and PSK31, use digital signals to transmit data over the airwaves. These modes can provide reliable and error-corrected data transmission over long distances.

Overall, digital circuits are becoming increasingly valuable and viable for use in ham radio. The use of digital circuits in ham radio systems is likely to continue to grow in importance as technology continues to evolve and new applications are developed.

Amplifiers and Oscillators

Amplifiers and oscillators are two fundamental types of circuits used in ham radio systems. **Amplifiers** are used to boost the strength of signals, while **oscillators** are used to generate signals at a particular frequency.

Amplifiers are an essential component of most ham radio systems and are tangentially involved with many of the other circuit components covered in this study guide. They are used to increase the strength of signals received from antennas or other sources, allowing weaker signals to be received and processed by the receiver. Amplifiers can also boost the power of signals transmitted by the transmitter, allowing signals to be transmitted over longer distances. With the right combination of equipment and favorable conditions, it is possible to achieve communication distances of several thousand miles or more.

Amplifiers can be designed using a variety of technologies, including vacuum tubes, bipolar junction transistors (BJTs), and field-effect transistors (FETs). Vacuum tube amplifiers are often used in high-power applications, such as amplifiers for HF transmitters, while solid-state amplifiers using BJTs and FETs are commonly used in low-power applications, such as preamplifiers and receivers.

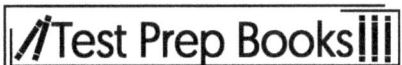

Oscillators, as explained in G6A: Inductors and G6A: Vacuum Tubes, are used in ham radio systems to generate signals at a particular frequency. The oscillator frequency is typically controlled by a resonant circuit, which consists of an inductor and a capacitor. The frequency of the oscillator can be adjusted by changing the values of the inductor and capacitor or by adjusting the voltage or current applied to the resonant circuit.

Oscillators can be designed using a variety of technologies, including LC oscillators, crystal oscillators, and phase-locked loop (PLL) oscillators. LC oscillators are simple, low-cost oscillators often used in low-frequency applications. Crystal oscillators are highly stable and accurate and are commonly used in high-frequency applications such as frequency standards and reference oscillators. PLL oscillators are used to generate highly stable, low-noise signals and are often used in frequency synthesis applications.

In addition to their individual uses, amplifiers and oscillators are often used together in ham radio systems to perform a variety of functions. For example, a transmitter may use an oscillator to generate a signal at a particular frequency, which is then amplified by a power amplifier before being transmitted through the antenna. In the receiver, a low-noise amplifier may be used to boost the strength of weak signals received by the antenna, followed by a mixer and oscillator to down-convert the signal to a lower frequency for further processing.

G7C

Transceiver Design

Transceiver design determines the radio's performance and capabilities in terms of transmitting and receiving signals. Transceivers are designed to integrate the functions of a transmitter and receiver into a single unit, allowing users to switch between modes quickly and easily.

Ham radio transceiver designs can vary significantly depending on the intended use and frequency range. They range from simple low-power devices used for short-range communication to complex high-power systems capable of transmitting signals over long distances. However, several key elements are common to most transceiver designs.

The transmitter section of a ham radio transceiver typically includes an oscillator, amplifier, and modulation circuitry. The oscillator generates the radio frequency (RF) carrier signal, which is then amplified to the desired power level by the amplifier. Modulation circuitry is used to modulate the RF signal with the voice or data signal being transmitted.

The receiver section of a ham radio transceiver is designed to receive and process incoming signals. It typically includes an amplifier, mixer, local oscillator, and demodulator. The amplifier boosts the strength of incoming signals, while the mixer combines the incoming signal with a local oscillator signal to produce an intermediate frequency (IF) signal that is easier to process. The demodulator circuitry extracts the voice or data signal from the modulated IF signal.

Other critical elements of ham radio transceiver design include filters, which are used to remove unwanted signals and interference from the received signal (outlined more in G7C: Oscillators), and signal processing circuitry, which is used to extract the voice or data signal from the modulated RF or IF signal.

Subelement G7 – Practical Circuits

Modern ham radio transceivers often incorporate digital signal processing (DSP) technology, which allows for advanced filtering and signal processing capabilities. DSP technology can be used to remove interference, enhance weak signals, and provide advanced features such as noise reduction and voice recording (outlined more in G7C: Digital Signal Processing (DSP)).

Transceiver design is also influenced by the frequency range of the radio. Lower frequency bands such as HF typically require larger antennas and longer wavelengths, which can affect the size and design of the transceiver. Higher frequency bands such as very high frequency (VHF) and ultra-high frequency (UHF) typically require smaller antennas and shorter wavelengths, which can allow for more compact and portable transceiver designs.

Filters

In ham radio systems, **filters** are used to remove unwanted frequencies and noise that can affect the quality of signals being transmitted and received, thereby playing a crucial role in optimizing communication efficiency.

One of the most common types of filters used in ham radio systems is the **band-pass filter**. A band-pass filter allows a specific frequency range to pass through while blocking all other frequencies. This type of filter is useful for isolating frequencies, which eliminates unwanted signals that are outside the frequency range of interest.

Another type of filter used in ham radio systems is the **low-pass filter**. A low-pass filter blocks all frequencies above a certain point, allowing only lower frequencies to pass through. This type of filter is useful for reducing high-frequency noise that can interfere with the clarity of voice or data signals.

Similarly, a **high-pass filter** blocks all frequencies below a certain point and allows only higher frequencies.

Oscillators

Oscillators are a critical component of ham radio systems, as they provide the basic signal transmitted or received by the radio. An oscillator generates an electrical signal that oscillates at a specific frequency and can be used to create a carrier wave that is modulated with voice or data to carry information over the airwaves.

The crystal oscillator is especially common among ham radio systems. Crystal oscillators use the piezoelectric effect of a quartz crystal to create a stable oscillation frequency. They are widely used because of their accuracy and stability, both of which are important for maintaining the integrity of signals transmitted and received by the radio.

Another type of oscillator used in ham radio systems is the voltage-controlled oscillator (VCO). A VCO's frequency can be adjusted by varying the input voltage, making it useful for frequency modulation (FM) or phase modulation (PM). VCOs are also used in frequency synthesizers, which can generate signals for different frequencies.

In addition to crystal and VCO oscillators, there are other types of oscillators used in ham radio systems, such as the Colpitts oscillator and the Hartley oscillator. These oscillators have different circuit designs and characteristics, but all provide a stable and reliable source of oscillation for transmitting and receiving signals in a ham radio system.

Digital Sign Processing (DSP)

A more modern innovation in radio technology, digital signal processing (DSP) (as mentioned in G7B: Digital Circuits), has revolutionized the way ham radio systems process and manipulate signals. DSP involves the use of mathematical algorithms to manipulate signals in digital form, which enables the extraction of useful information from noisy and degraded signals. As ham radio systems continue to evolve, DSP is likely to play an increasingly important role in their design and operation.

One of the most important applications of DSP in ham radio systems is signal filtering. DSP filters can be used to remove noise and unwanted signals, thus improving the clarity of received signals. DSP filters can also implement complex signal processing functions such as demodulation, decoding, and equalization.

DSP is particularly useful in modern ham radio systems, which often use software-defined radios (SDRs). SDRs use DSP to process and manipulate signals, rather than analog circuits. SDRs offer greater flexibility and versatility than traditional analog radios because they can be reconfigured and reprogrammed to handle different modes and frequencies.

DSP also improves ham radio systems through digital signal modulation. Digital modulation techniques such as phase-shift keying (PSK) and quadrature amplitude modulation (QAM) are used to encode digital data onto a carrier signal, enabling high-speed data transmission over the airwaves. DSP algorithms are used to generate and demodulate these digital signals, allowing for reliable and efficient data transmission.

Another way DSP is used in ham radio systems is to implement various signal processing functions, such as automatic gain control (AGC) and adaptive noise cancellation. AGC is a technique that automatically adjusts the gain of an amplifier to maintain a constant output level, even in the presence of varying input signal levels. Adaptive noise cancellation is a technique that uses DSP to cancel out unwanted noise in a signal and improve the signal-to-noise ratio.

Subelement G7 – Questions

G7A

1. What is the function of a power supply bleeder resistor?
    A. It acts as a fuse for excess voltage
    B. It discharges the filter capacitors when power is removed
    C. It removes shock hazards from the induction coils
    D. It eliminates ground loop current

2. Which of the following components are used in a power supply filter network?
    A. Diodes
    B. Transformers and transducers
    C. Capacitors and inductors
    D. All these choices are correct

3. Which type of rectifier circuit uses two diodes and a center-tapped transformer?
    A. Full-wave
    B. Full-wave bridge
    C. Half-wave
    D. Synchronous

4. What is characteristic of a half-wave rectifier in a power supply?
    A. Only one diode is required
    B. The ripple frequency is twice that of a full-wave rectifier
    C. More current can be drawn from the half-wave rectifier
    D. The output voltage is two times the peak input voltage

5. What portion of the AC cycle is converted to DC by a half-wave rectifier?
    A. 90 degrees
    B. 180 degrees
    C. 270 degrees
    D. 360 degrees

6. What portion of the AC cycle is converted to DC by a full-wave rectifier?
    A. 90 degrees
    B. 180 degrees
    C. 270 degrees
    D. 360 degrees

7. What is the output waveform of an unfiltered full-wave rectifier connected to a resistive load?
    A. A series of DC pulses at twice the frequency of the AC input
    B. A series of DC pulses at the same frequency as the AC input
    C. A sine wave at half the frequency of the AC input
    D. A steady DC voltage

8. Which of the following is characteristic of a switched-mode power supply as compared to a linear power supply?
    A. Faster switching time makes higher output voltage possible
    B. Fewer circuit components are required
    C. High-frequency operation allows the use of smaller components
    D. Inherently more stable

9. Which symbol in figure G7-1 represents a field effect transistor?
    A. Symbol 2
    B. Symbol 5
    C. Symbol 1
    D. Symbol 4

10. Which symbol in figure G7-1 represents a Zener diode?
    A. Symbol 4
    B. Symbol 1
    C. Symbol 11
    D. Symbol 5

11. Which symbol in figure G7-1 represents an NPN junction transistor?
    A. Symbol 1
    B. Symbol 2
    C. Symbol 7
    D. Symbol 11

12. Which symbol in Figure G7-1 represents a solid core transformer?
    A. Symbol 4
    B. Symbol 7
    C. Symbol 6
    D. Symbol 1

13. Which symbol in Figure G7-1 represents a tapped inductor?
    A. Symbol 7
    B. Symbol 11
    C. Symbol 6
    D. Symbol 1

G7B

1. What is the purpose of neutralizing an amplifier?
    A. To limit the modulation index
    B. To eliminate self-oscillations
    C. To cut off the final amplifier during standby periods
    D. To keep the carrier on frequency

2. Which of these classes of amplifiers has the highest efficiency?
   A. Class A
   B. Class B
   C. Class AB
   D. Class C

3. Which of the following describes the function of a two-input AND gate?
   A. Output is high when either or both inputs are low
   B. Output is high only when both inputs are high
   C. Output is low when either or both inputs are high
   D. Output is low only when both inputs are high

4. In a Class A amplifier, what percentage of the time does the amplifying device conduct?
   A. 100%
   B. More than 50% but less than 100%
   C. 50%
   D. Less than 50%

5. How many states does a 3-bit binary counter have?
   A. 3
   B. 6
   C. 8
   D. 16

6. What is a shift register?
   A. A clocked array of circuits that passes data in steps along the array
   B. An array of operational amplifiers used for tri-state arithmetic operations
   C. A digital mixer
   D. An analog mixer

7. Which of the following are basic components of a sine wave oscillator?
   A. An amplifier and a divider
   B. A frequency multiplier and a mixer
   C. A circulator and a filter operating in a feed-forward loop
   D. A filter and an amplifier operating in a feedback loop

8. How is the efficiency of an RF power amplifier determined?
   A. Divide the DC input power by the DC output power
   B. Divide the RF output power by the DC input power
   C. Multiply the RF input power by the reciprocal of the RF output power
   D. Add the RF input power to the DC output power

9. What determines the frequency of an LC oscillator?
   A. The number of stages in the counter
   B. The number of stages in the divider
   C. The inductance and capacitance in the tank circuit
   D. The time delay of the lag circuit

10. Which of the following describes a linear amplifier?
    A. Any RF power amplifier used in conjunction with an amateur transceiver
    B. An amplifier in which the output preserves the input waveform
    C. A Class C high efficiency amplifier
    D. An amplifier used as a frequency multiplier

11. For which of the following modes is a Class C power stage appropriate for amplifying a modulated signal?
    A. SSB
    B. FM
    C. AM
    D. All these choices are correct

G7C

1. What circuit is used to select one of the sidebands from a balanced modulator?
    A. Carrier oscillator
    B. Filter
    C. IF amplifier
    D. RF amplifier

2. What output is produced by a balanced modulator?
    A. Frequency modulated RF
    B. Audio with equalized frequency response
    C. Audio extracted from the modulation signal
    D. Double-sideband modulated RF

3. What is one reason to use an impedance matching transformer at a transmitter output?
    A. To minimize transmitter power output
    B. To present the desired impedance to the transmitter and feed line
    C. To reduce power supply ripple
    D. To minimize radiation resistance

4. How is a product detector used?
    A. Used in test gear to detect spurious mixing products
    B. Used in transmitter to perform frequency multiplication
    C. Used in an FM receiver to filter out unwanted sidebands
    D. Used in a single sideband receiver to extract the modulated signal

5. Which of the following is characteristic of a direct digital synthesizer (DDS)?
    A. Extremely narrow tuning range
    B. Relatively high-power output
    C. Pure sine wave output
    D. Variable output frequency with the stability of a crystal oscillator

6. Which of the following is an advantage of a digital signal processing (DSP) filter compared to an analog filter?
    A. A wide range of filter bandwidths and shapes can be created
    B. Fewer digital components are required
    C. Mixing products are greatly reduced
    D. The DSP filter is much more effective at VHF frequencies

7. What term specifies a filter's attenuation inside its passband?
    A. Insertion loss
    B. Return loss
    C. Q
    D. Ultimate rejection

8. Which parameter affects receiver sensitivity?
    A. Input amplifier gain
    B. Demodulator stage bandwidth
    C. Input amplifier noise figure
    D. All these choices are correct

9. What is the phase difference between the I and Q RF signals that software-defined radio (SDR) equipment uses for modulation and demodulation?
    A. Zero
    B. 90 degrees
    C. 180 degrees
    D. 45 degrees

10. What is an advantage of using I-Q modulation with software-defined radios (SDRs)?
    A. The need for high resolution analog-to-digital converters is eliminated
    B. All types of modulation can be created with appropriate processing
    C. Minimum detectible signal level is reduced
    D. Automatic conversion of the signal from digital to analog

11. Which of these functions is performed by software in a software-defined radio (SDR)?
    A. Filtering
    B. Detection
    C. Modulation
    D. All these choices are correct

12. What is the frequency above which a low-pass filter's output power is less than half the input power?
    A. Notch frequency
    B. Neper frequency
    C. Cutoff frequency
    D. Rolloff frequency

13. What term specifies a filter's maximum ability to reject signals outside its passband?
    A. Notch depth
    B. Rolloff
    C. Insertion loss
    D. Ultimate rejection

14. The bandwidth of a band-pass filter is measured between what two frequencies?
    A. Upper and lower half-power
    B. Cutoff and rolloff
    C. Pole and zero
    D. Image and harmonic

Subelement G7 – Answer Key

G7A

1. B	8. C
2. C	9. C
3. A	10. D
4. A	11. B
5. B	12. C
6. D	13. A
7. A	

G7B

1. B	7. D
2. D	8. B
3. B	9. C
4. A	10. B
5. C	11. B
6. A	

G7C

1. B	8. D
2. D	9. B
3. B	10. B
4. D	11. D
5. D	12. C
6. A	13. D
7. A	14. A

Subelement G8 – Signals and Emissions

G8A

Carriers and Modulation: AM, FM, and Single Sideband

Carriers and modulation are fundamental concepts in the world of radio communications. A carrier wave is a high-frequency wave that is modulated or changed to transmit information. The information is impressed onto the carrier wave by changing its amplitude, frequency, or phase. This process, called modulation, is used to transmit voice, data, images, or other forms of information. The modulation index refers to the ratio of the amplitude of the modulating signal to the amplitude of the carrier signal; it determines the degree of modulation. Excessive modulation can cause distortion of the signal.

The concept of carriers and modulation is critical to ham radio systems, as they use a variety of modulation techniques to transmit information over the airwaves. The three most common modulation techniques used in ham radio systems are **amplitude modulation (AM), frequency modulation (FM),** and **single sideband modulation (SSB).**

AM is a simple modulation technique that has been used since the early days of radio communications. It involves varying the amplitude of the carrier wave in proportion to the modulating signal. The modulating signal is usually a voice signal that is amplified and mixed with the carrier wave to produce an AM signal. The resulting signal produces two sidebands, which are symmetrically spaced around the carrier frequency. In radio communication, a sideband refers to a portion of a modulated signal that contains the information being transmitted.

AM signals have unique properties that make them more useful than FM signals in certain situations. For example, they are relatively easy to generate and detect, and they can be received on a wide range of equipment; in fact, older radio equipment is more likely to only support AM signals. However, AM signals are not very efficient in terms of bandwidth utilization, which limits the number of signals that can be transmitted simultaneously within a given frequency. In addition, since any variation in the amplitude of a signal, such as electrical noise or other sources of interference, can disrupt the signal's information, and that noise affects the amplitude of the signal, AM signals are particularly susceptible to noise and interference. AM signals are best used in devices and applications where simple, low-power equipment, long range, and/or the use of multiple stations on one channel are especially important, such as broadcast radio, amateur radio and military communications.

FM is another modulation technique that is widely used in ham radio systems. Whereas AM varies the amplitude of a carrier wave, FM involves varying the frequency of the carrier wave in proportion to the modulating signal. Like AM, however, the modulating signal used for FM is usually a voice signal, amplified and mixed with the carrier wave to modulate it, and the resulting signal remains a carrier frequency with two sidebands centered on it. But while AM signals produce only one pair of sidebands per frequency, FM signals produce an infinite amount of signal pairs and use only one at a time.

FM signals also have situational properties that make them preferable to AM signals in certain circumstances. For example, they are less susceptible to noise and interference than AM signals, and they can transmit multiple signals simultaneously. However, FM signals require more bandwidth than AM signals, and they are more complex to generate and detect. FM is useful in applications where a high-quality and low-interference signal is preferred, such as in commercial broadcast stations or mobile radio systems.

SSB modulation is a type of amplitude modulation that uses only one of the sidebands and fully suppresses the carrier wave. SSB modulation can be further classified into either USB or LSB modulation. The choice of sideband depends on the frequency band being used, and the convention is to use USB for frequencies above 10 MHz and LSB for frequencies below 10 MHz. The process of SSB modulation begins when an AM signal is generated. This signal is then passed through a filter that removes one of the sidebands and the carrier, resulting in an SSB signal. The filter used for this purpose is called a bandpass filter, and it typically has a uniquely narrow bandwidth. Once the SSB signal is generated, it is amplified and transmitted.

SSB modulation has several advantages over both AM and FM modulation. For example, it is the most efficient signal in terms of bandwidth use out of the three, and it can transmit more information in the same bandwidth. Additionally, SSB modulation is considerably less susceptible to noise and interference than AM or FM modulation due to its use of a narrower bandwidth, which makes it ideal for long-range communications.

SSB does have some significant disadvantages when compared to AM and FM, however, not the least of which is that it requires more sophisticated equipment to transmit and receive than either AM or FM, so it's generally less accessible. This is because SSB signals need to be demodulated and filtered in a way that preserves the original audio or data while rejecting the unwanted sideband and carrier. This requires more complex circuits and components than those needed for AM or FM, which makes SSB equipment more expensive and difficult to maintain. Additionally, SSB requires a higher level of skill and experience than Am or FM to use effectively. Because SSB signals are more sensitive to frequency drift and other signal distortions, adjusting and maintaining SSB transmission can be a particular challenge. This means that SSB may not be the best choice for novice or less experienced radio operators.

The choice of modulation technique is critical in ham radio systems, as it affects the quality and efficiency of the signal. Operators must carefully consider the application and available resources when choosing a modulation technique and adjust the transmission parameters accordingly to achieve the best results. Generally speaking, informed ham radio operators prefer AM modulation when long range is important or when using older equipment, FM modulation when signal quality takes priority, and SSB modulation when bandwidth efficiency and power retention are the priorities. Even though SSB is better at long range than AM, it is pointedly less accessible, and AM will often serve for most other ham radio functions.

Modulation Envelope

A **modulation envelope** is a graphical representation of the changes in the amplitude of a modulated signal over time. In ham radio systems, modulation envelopes are used to visualize and analyze the properties of amplitude modulated (AM) signals. When the amplitude of the carrier wave is modulated by the information signal, the modulation envelope represents the changes in amplitude.

A modulation envelope is a useful tool for analyzing AM signals because it provides information about the amplitude of the signal as it varies over time. This information can be used to determine the peak amplitude of the signal, the average amplitude of the signal, and the depth of modulation, which is the extent to which the amplitude of the carrier wave is varied by the information signal. The modulation envelope can be graphically represented by plotting the amplitude of the modulated signal on the y-axis

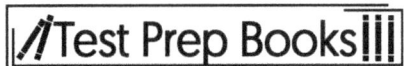

and time on the x-axis. The resulting waveform is a series of peaks and troughs that correspond to the variations in amplitude of the signal.

In addition to its use in analyzing AM signals, the modulation envelope can be used to measure the distortion of the modulated signal caused by various factors such as nonlinearities in the transmitter or receiver circuits, or interference from other signals. This is especially important for AM signals because they are more susceptible to this interference than FM or SSB signals.

Digital Modulation

Digital modulation refers to the process of encoding digital information onto an analog carrier signal to transmit it over a communication channel. In ham radio systems, digital modulation is becoming increasingly popular due to its ability to transmit data more efficiently and with greater accuracy than analog modulation techniques.

Digital modulation can be achieved through various methods, including **Amplitude Shift Keying (ASK)**, **Frequency Shift Keying (FSK)**, and **Phase Shift Keying (PSK)**. In **ASK**, the amplitude of the carrier signal is modulated to represent digital information. In **FSK**, that information is represented by modulating the carrier signal frequency, and in **PSK**, it is represented by modulating the phase of the carrier signal.

One of the key advantages of digital modulation is its ability to better resist noise and interference. Because digital signals consist of discrete values, they can be more easily reconstructed at the receiver end, even if the transmitted signal has been distorted or degraded by noise or interference. This makes digital modulation particularly well-suited for use in low signal-to-noise ratio environments, which are common in ham radio operations.

Additionally, digital modulation transmits data more efficiently than analog modulation, which limits the amount of data that can be transmitted by the available bandwidth of the communication channel. Digital modulation allows for higher data rates to be achieved within the same bandwidth, which makes it a more efficient means of transmitting information.

Overmodulation

Overmodulation is a phenomenon that occurs when the amplitude of the modulating signal exceeds the maximum level that can be accommodated by the modulation process, resulting in distortion of the transmitted signal. Overmodulation can occur in all three forms of modulation, which are explained in detail in "G8A: Carriers and modulation: AM, FM, and single sideband."

In AM modulation, overmodulation occurs when the modulation depth exceeds 100 percent, which means that the amplitude of the modulating signal is greater than the carrier signal. This causes the amplitude of the carrier signal to be distorted and results in the production of harmonics and intermodulation products that can interfere with adjacent frequency channels.

In FM modulation, overmodulation is caused by the frequency deviation exceeding the maximum allowed frequency deviation, which is determined by the frequency deviation sensitivity of the receiver. This causes the signal to become wider in bandwidth and may cause adjacent channel interference.

In SSB modulation, overmodulation occurs when the modulating signal exceeds the maximum level allowed by the transmitter. This usually results in distortion of the transmitted signal and the generation of unwanted sideband products.

Subelement G8 – Signals and Emissions

To prevent overmodulation, set modulation levels properly to ensure that the amplitude or frequency deviation of the modulating signal does not exceed the maximum allowable level.

Link Budgets and Margins

A **link budget** is a mathematical calculation used to determine the total gain or loss of a signal as it travels from the transmitter to the receiver. It takes into account all of the factors that can affect the strength of the signal, including the transmitting power, the antenna gain, the cable losses, and the path loss due to distance and obstacles. The link budget can be used to determine whether a given radio link will be able to meet the required signal strength at the receiver, which is known as the minimum received signal level.

The **link margin**, on the other hand, is the difference between the actual received signal level and the minimum required signal level. It represents the amount of extra signal strength that is available to account for any unexpected losses or interference that may occur in the system. The link margin is usually expressed in decibels (dB). A higher link margin means a more robust and reliable radio link.

Various factors must be considered to calculate the link budget. These include the transmitting power, antenna gain, cable losses, and path loss. The transmitting power refers to the strength of the signal at the output of the transmitter, and it is typically measured in watts (W) or decibels relative to a milliwatt (dBm). The antenna gain is a measure of the directionality of the antenna and is also measured in decibels.

Once the link budget is calculated, the link margin can be determined by subtracting the minimum required signal level from the actual received signal level. The link margin can be used to ensure that the radio link is robust and reliable, even in adverse conditions.

G8B

Frequency Changing

Frequency changing, also known as frequency shifting or frequency conversion, is a technique commonly used to manipulate the frequency of radio signals. It involves altering the frequency of a radio signal to a different frequency in order to facilitate communication over long distances.

In ham radio systems, frequency changing is achieved using devices called mixers. A mixer combines two input signals, which are usually at different frequencies, to produce an output signal at a new frequency equal to the sum or difference of the input frequencies. The process of combining two signals is known as heterodyning, and the output signal is called an intermediate frequency (IF) signal.

One of the main reasons for frequency changing in ham radio systems is to enable communication over long distances. High-frequency (HF) signals, which are commonly used in ham radio, can travel great distances by bouncing off the ionosphere, but they are also susceptible to interference and attenuation. A ham radio operator can use frequency changing to select a specific frequency that is more conducive to long-distance communication, and then convert the signal to a different frequency that is less prone to interference.

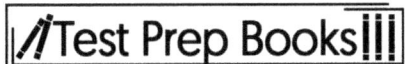

Subelement G8 – Signals and Emissions

Frequency changing is also useful for signal processing. A ham radio operator can use a mixer to shift the frequency of a radio signal to filter out unwanted frequencies, amplify weak signals, or even demodulate signals that have been modulated onto a carrier frequency. Frequency changing is therefore an essential tool for many of the signal processing techniques used in ham radio systems, including filtering, amplification, and demodulation.

Frequency changing is also used in many types of ham radio equipment, including transceivers, receivers, and transmitters. Transceivers, which are used for two-way communication, typically employ a mixer to convert the frequency of the received signal to an IF frequency, and then convert the frequency of the transmitted signal to the desired frequency for transmission. Receivers use a mixer to convert the received signal to an IF frequency, which is then amplified and demodulated. Transmitters use a mixer to generate a carrier signal at the desired frequency, which is then modulated with the information signal and amplified for transmission.

Bandwidths of Various Modes

Different modes of radio signals use different bandwidths. The bandwidth of a transmission is the range of frequencies the signal occupies. It is important to understand the bandwidth of various modes because this determines how much space on the frequency spectrum is required for the transmission, and whether the transmission will interfere with other signals.

AM (amplitude modulation) is one of the oldest forms of modulation used in radio communications. The bandwidth of an AM signal is twice the maximum frequency of the modulating signal. For example, if the highest frequency in the audio being transmitted is 3 kHz, the bandwidth of the AM signal will be 6 kHz. The bandwidth of an AM signal is relatively wide, and as a result, it is not an efficient use of the frequency spectrum.

FM (frequency modulation) is a more efficient modulation technique than AM, as it uses a narrower bandwidth. The bandwidth of an FM signal is determined by the frequency deviation, which is the maximum difference between the carrier frequency and the modulating frequency. The bandwidth of an FM signal can be calculated using Carson's rule, which states that the bandwidth is approximately twice the sum of the frequency deviation and the maximum modulating frequency. For example, if the maximum frequency deviation is 5 kHz and the highest modulating frequency is 3 kHz, the bandwidth of the FM signal would be approximately 16 kHz.

Single Sideband (SSB) is a form of amplitude modulation that is more efficient than traditional AM, as it uses a narrower bandwidth. SSB transmission only uses one of the two sidebands, and the carrier is suppressed. This reduces the bandwidth of the transmission to approximately half that of AM. SSB is often used in long-distance communication and is the preferred mode for many ham radio operators.

Digital modes such as PSK31, RTTY, and JT65 use very narrow bandwidths, typically less than 1 kHz. These modes use digital modulation techniques to transmit data, and the signals are usually very weak. These narrow bandwidths are ideal for weak signal communication and allow for many signals to occupy the same frequency band.

Deviation

Deviation describes the extent to which the frequency of an FM signal varies in response to changes in the amplitude of the modulating signal. Essentially, deviation refers to the amount by which the

Subelement G8 – Signals and Emissions

frequency of an FM signal is modulated or changed in response to the signal being transmitted. In an FM radio signal, the carrier frequency remains constant, but the frequency of the signal is modulated by the audio signal being transmitted. The amount of deviation in the signal is controlled by the modulating signal and determines the amount of bandwidth that is required for the transmission.

Deviation in an FM signal can be measured in several ways, including via a frequency counter or spectrum analyzer. In addition, some ham radio systems may include automatic deviation control (ADC) circuits, which help to maintain the deviation within the allowed limits.

Intermodulation

Intermodulation is a type of radio frequency interference that occurs when two or more signals mix together in a non-linear circuit or device, resulting in the creation of additional, unwanted signals. In ham radio systems, intermodulation can occur when two or more signals are in close proximity to each other and interact in a non-linear way that results in unwanted signals at frequencies that are not part of the original signals.

Operators can minimize intermodulation by using high-quality filters and isolators to prevent signals from mixing together in non-linear devices. Additionally, it is important to ensure that transmitter power levels are kept within legal limits, and that signals are properly spaced out to avoid interference.

G8C

Digital Emission Modes

Digital emission modes are a category of radio communication modes that use digital modulation techniques to transmit data over radio waves. These modes have gained popularity among amateur radio operators due to their efficient use of bandwidth and their ability to provide reliable communication in weak signal conditions.

Several types of digital emission modes are used in ham radio systems, each with its own unique characteristics and advantages. Below are some of the most common digital modes:

- **PSK**: **Phase shift keying** is a modulation scheme in which the phase of the carrier wave is varied to represent digital data. PSK is highly efficient and can provide reliable communication in weak signal conditions.

- **RTTY**: **Radio teletype** uses frequency shift keying (FSK) to transmit text messages over the airwaves. RTTY is commonly used in contesting and emergency communications due to its fast transmission rates and reliable performance.

- **JT65**: JT65 is a highly efficient digital mode that was developed for weak signal communication. It uses a sophisticated error-correcting code to ensure accurate data transmission even in conditions of high noise and interference.

- **FT8**: FT8 was developed for weak signal communication on HF bands. It uses a highly efficient modulation scheme and can reliably transmit data in conditions where other modes may fail.

Digital emission modes are highly efficient and can provide reliable communication even under weak signal conditions. They are particularly resistant to noise and interference, which makes them an excellent choice for amateur radio operators looking to make contact over long distances.

However, digital modes require specialized software and equipment to decode and encode the digital signals. This means beginners may find it more difficult to get started with digital modes compared to more traditional modes like voice or CW. In addition, some digital modes can be more challenging to set up and configure compared to others. For example, modes like JT65 require precise timing synchronization between the transmitting and receiving stations, which can be difficult to achieve without specialized equipment.

Subelement G8 - Questions

G8A

1. How is direct binary FSK modulation generated?
    A. By keying an FM transmitter with a sub-audible tone
    B. By changing an oscillator's frequency directly with a digital control signal
    C. By using a transceiver's computer data interface protocol to change frequencies
    D. By reconfiguring the CW keying input to act as a tone generator

2. What is the name of the process that changes the phase angle of an RF signal to convey information?
    A. Phase convolution
    B. Phase modulation
    C. Phase transformation
    D. Phase inversion

3. What is the name of the process that changes the instantaneous frequency of an RF wave to convey information?
    A. Frequency convolution
    B. Frequency transformation
    C. Frequency conversion
    D. Frequency modulation

4. What emission is produced by a reactance modulator connected to a transmitter RF amplifier stage?
    A. Multiplex modulation
    B. Phase modulation
    C. Amplitude modulation
    D. Pulse modulation

5. What type of modulation varies the instantaneous power level of the RF signal?
    A. Power modulation
    B. Phase modulation
    C. Frequency modulation
    D. Amplitude modulation

6. Which of the following is characteristic of QPSK31?
    A. It is sideband sensitive
    B. Its encoding provides error correction
    C. Its bandwidth is approximately the same as BPSK31
    D. All these choices are correct

7. Which of the following phone emissions uses the narrowest bandwidth?
    A. Single sideband
    B. Vestigial sideband
    C. Phase modulation
    D. Frequency modulation

8. Which of the following is an effect of overmodulation?
   A. Insufficient audio
   B. Insufficient bandwidth
   C. Frequency drift
   D. Excessive bandwidth

9. What type of modulation is used by FT8?
   A. 8-tone frequency shift keying
   B. Vestigial sideband
   C. Amplitude compressed AM
   D. 8-bit direct sequence spread spectrum

10. What is meant by the term "flat-topping," when referring to an amplitude-modulated phone signal?
    A. Signal distortion caused by insufficient collector current
    B. The transmitter's automatic level control (ALC) is properly adjusted
    C. Signal distortion caused by excessive drive or speech levels
    D. The transmitter's carrier is properly suppressed

11. What is the modulation envelope of an AM signal?
    A. The waveform created by connecting the peak values of the modulated signal
    B. The carrier frequency that contains the signal
    C. Spurious signals that envelop nearby frequencies
    D. The bandwidth of the modulated signal

12. What is QPSK modulation?
    A. Modulation using quasi-parallel to serial conversion to reduce bandwidth
    B. Modulation using quadra-pole sideband keying to generate spread spectrum signals
    C. Modulation using Fast Fourier Transforms to generate frequencies at the first, second, third, and fourth harmonics of the carrier frequency to improve noise immunity
    D. Modulation in which digital data is transmitted using 0-, 90-, 180- and 270-degrees phase shift to represent pairs of bits

13. What is a link budget?
    A. The financial costs associated with operating a radio link
    B. The sum of antenna gains minus system losses
    C. The sum of transmit power and antenna gains minus system losses as seen at the receiver
    D. The difference between transmit power and receiver sensitivity

14. What is link margin?
    A. The opposite of fade margin
    B. The difference between received power level and minimum required signal level at the input to the receiver
    C. Transmit power minus receiver sensitivity
    D. Receiver sensitivity plus 3 dB

G8B

1. Which mixer input is varied or tuned to convert signals of different frequencies to an intermediate frequency (IF)?
    A. Image frequency
    B. Local oscillator
    C. RF input
    D. Beat frequency oscillator

2. What is the term for interference from a signal at twice the IF frequency from the desired signal?
    A. Quadrature response
    B. Image response
    C. Mixer interference
    D. Intermediate interference

3. What is another term for the mixing of two RF signals?
    A. Heterodyning
    B. Synthesizing
    C. Frequency inversion
    D. Phase inversion

4. What is the stage in a VHF FM transmitter that generates a harmonic of a lower frequency signal to reach the desired operating frequency?
    A. Mixer
    B. Reactance modulator
    C. Balanced converter
    D. Multiplier

5. Which intermodulation products are closest to the original signal frequencies?
    A. Second harmonics
    B. Even-order
    C. Odd-order
    D. Intercept point

6. What is the total bandwidth of an FM phone transmission having 5 kHz deviation and 3 kHz modulating frequency?
    A. 3 kHz
    B. 5 kHz
    C. 8 kHz
    D. 16 kHz

7. What is the frequency deviation for a 12.21 MHz reactance modulated oscillator in a 5 kHz deviation, 146.52 MHz FM phone transmitter?
    A. 101.75 Hz
    B. 416.7 Hz
    C. 5 kHz
    D. 60 kHz

8. Why is it important to know the duty cycle of the mode you are using when transmitting?
    A. To aid in tuning your transmitter
    B. Some modes have high duty cycles that could exceed the transmitter's average power rating
    C. To allow time for the other station to break in during a transmission
    D. To prevent overmodulation

9. Why is it good to match receiver bandwidth to the bandwidth of the operating mode?
    A. It is required by FCC rules
    B. It minimizes power consumption in the receiver
    C. It improves impedance matching of the antenna
    D. It results in the best signal-to-noise ratio

10. What is the relationship between transmitted symbol rate and bandwidth?
    A. Symbol rate and bandwidth are not related
    B. Higher symbol rates require wider bandwidth
    C. Lower symbol rates require wider bandwidth
    D. Bandwidth is half the symbol rate

11. What combination of a mixer's Local Oscillator (LO) and RF input frequencies is found in the output?
    A. The ratio
    B. The average
    C. The sum and difference
    D. The arithmetic product

12. What process combines two signals in a non-linear circuit to produce unwanted spurious outputs?
    A. Intermodulation
    B. Heterodyning
    C. Detection
    D. Rolloff

13. Which of the following is an odd-order intermodulation product of frequencies F1 and F2?
    A. 5F1-3F2
    B. 3F1-F2
    C. 2F1-F2
    D. All these choices are correct

G8C

1. On what band do amateurs share channels with the unlicensed Wi-Fi service?
    A. 432 MHz
    B. 902 MHz
    C. 2.4 GHz
    D. 10.7 GHz

2. Which digital mode is used as a low-power beacon for assessing HF propagation?
    A. WSPR
    B. MFSK16
    C. PSK31
    D. SSB-SC

3. What part of a packet radio frame contains the routing and handling information?
    A. Directory
    B. Preamble
    C. Header
    D. Trailer

4. Which of the following describes Baudot code?
    A. A 7-bit code with start, stop, and parity bits
    B. A code using error detection and correction
    C. A 5-bit code with additional start and stop bits
    D. A code using SELCAL and LISTEN

5. In an ARQ mode, what is meant by a NAK response to a transmitted packet?
    A. Request retransmission of the packet
    B. Packet was received without error
    C. Receiving station connected and ready for transmissions
    D. Entire file received correctly

6. What action results from a failure to exchange information due to excessive transmission attempts when using an ARQ mode?
    A. The checksum overflows
    B. The connection is dropped
    C. Packets will be routed incorrectly
    D. Encoding reverts to the default character set

7. Which of the following narrow-band digital modes can receive signals with very low signal-to-noise ratios?
    A. MSK144
    B. FT8
    C. AMTOR
    D. MFSK32

8. Which of the following statements is true about PSK31?
    A. Upper case letters are sent with more power
    B. Upper case letters use longer Varicode bit sequences and thus slow down transmission
    C. Error correction is used to ensure accurate message reception
    D. Higher power is needed as compared to RTTY for similar error rates

9. Which is true of mesh network microwave nodes?
    A. Having more nodes increases signal strengths
    B. If one node fails, a packet may still reach its target station via an alternate node
    C. Links between two nodes in a network may have different frequencies and bandwidths
    D. More nodes reduce overall microwave out of band interference

10. How does forward error correction (FEC) allow the receiver to correct data errors?
    A. By controlling transmitter output power for optimum signal strength
    B. By using the Varicode character set
    C. By transmitting redundant information with the data
    D. By using a parity bit with each character

11. How are the two separate frequencies of a Frequency Shift Keyed (FSK) signal identified?
    A. Dot and dash
    B. On and off
    C. High and low
    D. Mark and space

12. Which type of code is used for sending characters in a PSK31 signal?
    A. Varicode
    B. Viterbi
    C. Volumetric
    D. Binary

13. What is indicated on a waterfall display by one or more vertical lines on either side of a data mode or RTTY signal?
    A. Long path propagation
    B. Backscatter propagation
    C. Insufficient modulation
    D. Overmodulation

14. Which of the following describes a waterfall display?
    A. Frequency is horizontal, signal strength is vertical, time is intensity
    B. Frequency is vertical, signal strength is intensity, time is horizontal
    C. Frequency is horizontal, signal strength is intensity, time is vertical
    D. Frequency is vertical, signal strength is horizontal, time is intensity

15. What does an FT8 signal report of +3 mean?
    A. The signal is 3 times the noise level of an equivalent SSB signal
    B. The signal is S3 (weak signals)
    C. The signal-to-noise ratio is equivalent to +3dB in a 2.5 kHz bandwidth
    D. The signal is 3 dB over S9

16. Which of the following provide digital voice modes?
    A. WSPR, MFSK16, and EasyPAL
    B. FT8, FT4, and FST4
    C. Winlink, PACTOR II, and PACTOR III
    D. DMR, D-STAR, and SystemFusion

Subelement G8 – Answer Key

G8A

1. B	8. D
2. B	9. A
3. D	10. C
4. B	11. A
5. D	12. D
6. D	13. C
7. A	14. B

G8B

1. B	8. B
2. B	9. D
3. A	10. B
4. D	11. C
5. C	12. A
6. D	13. C
7. B	

G8C

1. C	9. B
2. A	10. C
3. C	11. D
4. C	12. A
5. A	13. D
6. B	14. C
7. B	15. C
8. B	16. D

Subelement G9 – Antennas and Feed Lines

G9A

Feed lines: Characteristic Impedance and Attenuation

Feed lines are essential radio components that transfer RF energy between the transmitter, antenna, and receiver. The two primary parameters that characterize feed lines are characteristic impedance and attenuation.

Characteristic impedance is the impedance of the feed line measured in ohms at a given frequency. It is a measure of the opposition to the flow of RF energy due to the properties of the transmission line. The characteristic impedance of a feed line is a critical parameter because it determines the degree of signal reflection that occurs at the interface between the feed line and the antenna or transmitter. If the characteristic impedance of the feed line is not matched to the impedance of the antenna or transmitter, the reflected signal may cause standing waves, which reduces the efficiency of the system and causes signal loss.

Attenuation is the measure of signal loss over a given distance of feed line. As RF energy travels through the feed line, it encounters resistance due to the properties of the line, resulting in signal loss. The attenuation of a feed line is typically measured in decibels per unit length (dB/ft or dB/m) and varies with frequency, line type, and length. It is important to select a feed line that has low attenuation to minimize signal loss, especially over longer distances.

Standing Wave Ratio (SWR) Calculation, Measurement, and Effects

Standing wave ratio (SWR) is an important factor in the performance of many radio systems. SWR refers to the ratio of maximum to minimum amplitude of the standing wave pattern that occurs on a transmission line, which is also known as the feedline. A high SWR value indicates that there is a mismatch between the antenna and the transmission line, which can result in the degradation of the signal.

Calculating SWR involves measuring the reflected power on the radio transmission line. A directional coupler or SWR meter can be used to measure the forward and reflected power. The SWR is then calculated using the following formula: SWR = $(1 + \sqrt{(PRF/PFW)})/(1 - \sqrt{(PRF/PFW)})$, where PRF is the reflected power and PFW is the forward power.

The measurement of SWR is crucial in ensuring that the radio system operates at its maximum efficiency. A high SWR value indicates that there is a mismatch between the antenna and the transmission line, which can lead to signal loss and lasting damage to the radio equipment. A low SWR value indicates that the antenna and transmission line are well-matched, which results in better overall performance of the radio system.

A popular way to measure the SWR is to use an SWR meter, which can be either purchased separately or built into the radio equipment. An SWR meter measures the forward and reflected power, and the SWR is displayed on a meter or digital readout.

Subelement G9 – Antennas and Feed Lines

The effects of SWR on a ham radio system are significant. A high SWR value can cause significant signal loss, which can lead to poor signal quality and reduced communication range. It can also lead to damage to the radio equipment, particularly the transmitter. The reflected power can also cause damage to the final amplifier stages of the transmitter, which may be quite costly to repair.

In addition, high SWR values can cause problems with the automatic protection circuits in the radio equipment. The circuits are designed to protect the equipment from high reflected power levels, but if the SWR is consistently high, the protection circuits may trigger and lead to reduced power output and a reduction in performance.

Antenna Feed Point Matching

The objective of **feed point matching** is to ensure that the impedance of the antenna matches the impedance of the transmission line and the transmitter/receiver. If the impedance is not matched, there will be a mismatch loss, which can lead to a weaker signal, higher SWR, and interference. This can also damage the transmitter or receiver.

Impedance is a measure of the resistance to the flow of current in a circuit. The unit of impedance is ohms (Ω). The impedance of the antenna depends on the frequency of the signal being transmitted or received. Impedance can be expressed as a complex number with both a real (resistive) and imaginary (reactive) component. The resistive component is the actual resistance in the circuit, while the reactive component is the phase shift between the current and voltage in the circuit.

One of the most common ways to match the impedance of the feed line to the antenna is to use an impedance matching network, also known as an antenna tuner. An antenna tuner can be a simple LC circuit or a more complex automatic tuner. The tuner adjusts the impedance of the antenna to match the impedance of the feed line and transmitter/receiver. Another way to match the impedance is to use a balun, which is short for "balanced to unbalanced." A balun is a device that converts a balanced signal, such as that coming from a dipole antenna, to an unbalanced signal, which is what most feed lines and transmitters/receivers require. The balun also helps to prevent common-mode currents from flowing on the feed line, which can lead to interference and damage to the transmitter or receiver.

The length of the feed line can also affect the impedance matching. The impedance of the feed line changes with the length of the line and the frequency of the signal. For this reason, it is essential to use the correct length of feed line for the frequency.

In addition to matching the impedance, it is also crucial to ensure that the antenna is resonant at the desired frequency. A resonant antenna has an impedance that is purely resistive, meaning there is no reactive component. This helps to minimize mismatch losses and interference.

G9B

Basic Dipole and Monopole Antennae

Antennae are responsible for transmitting and receiving radio signals. Dipole and monopole antennae are the common types of antennae used in ham radio systems.

A **dipole antenna** is a simple and effective antenna design consisting of two equal-length conductive elements, which are typically oriented horizontally and parallel to the ground. The two elements are

typically connected to a transmission line, which is used to connect the antenna to the radio. When a signal is transmitted or received, it creates an electric current in the antenna elements, which in turn produces an electromagnetic field that radiates the signal out into space.

A **monopole antenna**, also known as a **quarter-wave vertical antenna**, is another common antenna design used in ham radio systems. Unlike a dipole antenna, a monopole antenna only has a single conductive element. This element is typically oriented vertically and connected to a ground plane. The ground plane can be either a large metal plate or a network of wires buried in the ground. When a signal is transmitted or received, the ground plane serves as the other half of the antenna and allows the signal to be radiated out into space.

One advantage of a dipole antenna over a monopole antenna is that it is usually more efficient, meaning more of the power from the transmitter is radiated out into space. This is because a dipole antenna has two conductive elements, which allows it to create a more symmetrical and uniform electromagnetic field. However, a dipole antenna also requires more space and is more difficult to install than a monopole antenna. A monopole antenna is usually easier to install because it only requires a single conductive element and a ground plane. Additionally, a monopole antenna is less affected by nearby objects such as buildings and trees, which can cause reflections and distortions in the electromagnetic field.

G9C

Directional Antennae

Directional antennae, also known as **beam antennae**, are a type of antenna that focus radio signals in a specific direction. They are commonly used to increase the gain and reduce the noise level of a signal. Directional antennae have a higher forward gain than other types of antennae and can help concentrate the signal in a specific direction, increasing the signal strength and improving communication.

One of the most common types of directional antennae used in ham radio systems is the **Yagi-Uda antenna**. The Yagi-Uda antenna is made up of a series of parallel dipole elements; one dipole is the driven element, and the others act as directors or reflectors. The driven element is connected to the radio transmitter, and the other elements are arranged in a specific pattern to produce a directional signal.

Another type of directional antenna commonly used in ham radio systems is the **log-periodic antenna**: a multi-element antenna that is designed to operate over a wide frequency range. It consists of a series of dipole elements of varying lengths that are arranged in a specific pattern to produce a directional signal. The log-periodic antenna is commonly used for HF and VHF frequencies, where it can provide gain and directional properties over a wide range of frequencies.

The directional antenna offers several advantages over other types of antennae. One primary advantage is its high gain, which allows for increased signal strength and better communication. The directional antenna also has a narrower beamwidth, which can help reduce interference from unwanted signals and noise. This makes it particularly useful in crowded or noisy environments where many other radio signals are present. However, directional antennae also come with disadvantages, one of which is that they are designed to focus radio signals in a specific direction. This can limit their usefulness for communications with stations located in different directions. Additionally, directional antennae tend to be larger and more complex than other types of antennae, which can make them more difficult to install and maintain.

G9D

Specialized Antenna Types and Applications

In addition to basic dipole, monopole, and directional antennae, many specialized antenna and antenna system types are used in ham radio systems for specific applications. Below are a few examples:

- **Loop antennae**: Though they are also technically directional antennae, loop antennae are typically smaller and can be used at lower frequencies. They are commonly used for portable or mobile operations, and can be constructed in various shapes, including circular or square. They are particularly useful for reducing interference from unwanted directions.

- **Vertical arrays**: A vertical array is a group of vertical antennae arranged in a specific pattern to achieve a particular radiation pattern. This technique can be used to achieve directional gain, reduce noise, or achieve other objectives. Vertical arrays are commonly used in the low-frequency bands for both transmitting and receiving.

- **Helical antennae**: These antennae are for circular polarization and are often used for satellite communications or other applications requiring circular polarization. They can also be used for terrestrial communications on VHF or UHF bands.

    - **Beverage antennae**: These long, directional antennae are designed for receiving low-frequency signals, typically below 2 MHz. They tend to be very long and narrow, often over 100 meters long. These antennae can provide good gain and directionality and are particularly useful for low-frequency DXing.

- **Discone antennae**: Discone antennae are used for wideband frequency reception or transmission, typically covering the frequency range from 30 MHz to 3 GHz or higher. They have a wide bandwidth and omnidirectional radiation pattern, which makes them useful for monitoring or scanning multiple frequencies simultaneously.

These are just a few examples of the many specialized antenna types used in ham radio systems, though the ones listed above are some of the most common. Each type has its own unique design and use, and choosing the right antenna for the right application can significantly improve the performance of a ham radio system.

Subelement G9 – Questions

G9A

1. Which of the following factors determine the characteristic impedance of a parallel conductor feed line?
    A. The distance between the centers of the conductors and the radius of the conductors
    B. The distance between the centers of the conductors and the length of the line
    C. The radius of the conductors and the frequency of the signal
    D. The frequency of the signal and the length of the line

2. What is the relationship between high standing wave ratio (SWR) and transmission line loss?
    A. There is no relationship between transmission line loss and SWR
    B. High SWR increases loss in a lossy transmission line
    C. High SWR makes it difficult to measure transmission line loss
    D. High SWR reduces the relative effect of transmission line loss

3. What is the nominal characteristic impedance of "window line" transmission line?
    A. 50 ohms
    B. 75 ohms
    C. 100 ohms
    D. 450 ohms

4. What causes reflected power at an antenna's feed point?
    A. Operating an antenna at its resonant frequency
    B. Using more transmitter power than the antenna can handle
    C. A difference between feed line impedance and antenna feed point impedance
    D. Feeding the antenna with unbalanced feed line

5. How does the attenuation of coaxial cable change with increasing frequency?
    A. Attenuation is independent of frequency
    B. Attenuation increases
    C. Attenuation decreases
    D. Attenuation follows Marconi's Law of Attenuation

6. In what units is RF feed line loss usually expressed?
    A. Ohms per 1,000 feet
    B. Decibels per 1,000 feet
    C. Ohms per 100 feet
    D. Decibels per 100 feet

7. What must be done to prevent standing waves on a feed line connected to an antenna?
    A. The antenna feed point must be at DC ground potential
    B. The feed line must be an odd number of electrical quarter wavelengths long
    C. The feed line must be an even number of physical half wavelengths long
    D. The antenna feed point impedance must be matched to the characteristic impedance of the feed line

Subelement G9 – Antennas and Feed Lines

8. If the SWR on an antenna feed line is 5:1, and a matching network at the transmitter end of the feed line is adjusted to present a 1:1 SWR to the transmitter, what is the resulting SWR on the feed line?
    A. 1:1
    B. 5:1
    C. Between 1:1 and 5:1 depending on the characteristic impedance of the line
    D. Between 1:1 and 5:1 depending on the reflected power at the transmitter

9. What standing wave ratio results from connecting a 50-ohm feed line to a 200-ohm resistive load?
    A. 4:1
    B. 1:4
    C. 2:1
    D. 1:2

10. What standing wave ratio results from connecting a 50-ohm feed line to a 10-ohm resistive load?
    A. 2:1
    B. 1:2
    C. 1:5
    D. 5:1

11. What is the effect of transmission line loss on SWR measured at the input to the line?
    A. Higher loss reduces SWR measured at the input to the line
    B. Higher loss increases SWR measured at the input to the line
    C. Higher loss increases the accuracy of SWR measured at the input to the line
    D. Transmission line loss does not affect the SWR measurement

G9B

1. What is a characteristic of a random-wire HF antenna connected directly to the transmitter?
    A. It must be longer than 1 wavelength
    B. Station equipment may carry significant RF current
    C. It produces only vertically polarized radiation
    D. It is more effective on the lower HF bands than on the higher bands

2. Which of the following is a common way to adjust the feed point impedance of an elevated quarter-wave ground-plane vertical antenna to be approximately 50 ohms?
    A. Slope the radials upward
    B. Slope the radials downward
    C. Lengthen the radials beyond one wavelength
    D. Coil the radials

3. Which of the following best describes the radiation pattern of a quarter-wave ground-plane vertical antenna?
    A. Bi-directional in azimuth
    B. Isotropic
    C. Hemispherical
    D. Omnidirectional in azimuth

4. What is the radiation pattern of a dipole antenna in free space in a plane containing the conductor?
    A. It is a figure-eight at right angles to the antenna
    B. It is a figure-eight off both ends of the antenna
    C. It is a circle (equal radiation in all directions)
    D. It has a pair of lobes on one side of the antenna and a single lobe on the other side

5. How does antenna height affect the azimuthal radiation pattern of a horizontal dipole HF antenna at elevation angles higher than about 45 degrees?
    A. If the antenna is too high, the pattern becomes unpredictable
    B. Antenna height has no effect on the pattern
    C. If the antenna is less than 1/2 wavelength high, the azimuthal pattern is almost omnidirectional
    D. If the antenna is less than 1/2 wavelength high, radiation off the ends of the wire is eliminated

6. Where should the radial wires of a ground-mounted vertical antenna system be placed?
    A. As high as possible above the ground
    B. Parallel to the antenna element
    C. On the surface or buried a few inches below the ground
    D. At the center of the antenna

7. How does the feed point impedance of a horizontal 1/2 wave dipole antenna change as the antenna height is reduced to 1/10 wavelength above ground?
    A. It steadily increases
    B. It steadily decreases
    C. It peaks at about 1/8 wavelength above ground
    D. It is unaffected by the height above ground

8. How does the feed point impedance of a 1/2 wave dipole change as the feed point is moved from the center toward the ends?
    A. It steadily increases
    B. It steadily decreases
    C. It peaks at about 1/8 wavelength from the end
    D. It is unaffected by the location of the feed point

9. Which of the following is an advantage of using a horizontally polarized as compared to a vertically polarized HF antenna?
    A. Lower ground losses
    B. Lower feed point impedance
    C. Shorter radials
    D. Lower radiation resistance

10. What is the approximate length for a 1/2 wave dipole antenna cut for 14.250 MHz?
    A. 8 feet
    B. 16 feet
    C. 24 feet
    D. 33 feet

Subelement G9 – Antennas and Feed Lines

11. What is the approximate length for a 1/2 wave dipole antenna cut for 3.550 MHz?
    A. 42 feet
    B. 84 feet
    C. 132 feet
    D. 263 feet

12. What is the approximate length for a 1/4 wave monopole antenna cut for 28.5 MHz?
    A. 8 feet
    B. 11 feet
    C. 16 feet
    D. 21 feet

G9C

1. Which of the following would increase the bandwidth of a Yagi antenna?
    A. Larger-diameter elements
    B. Closer element spacing
    C. Loading coils in series with the element
    D. Tapered-diameter elements

2. What is the approximate length of the driven element of a Yagi antenna?
    A. 1/4 wavelength
    B. 1/2 wavelength
    C. 3/4 wavelength
    D. 1 wavelength

3. How do the lengths of a three-element Yagi reflector and director compare to that of the driven element?
    A. The reflector is longer, and the director is shorter
    B. The reflector is shorter, and the director is longer
    C. They are all the same length
    D. Relative length depends on the frequency of operation

4. How does antenna gain in dBi compare to gain stated in dBd for the same antenna?
    A. Gain in dBi is 2.15 dB lower
    B. Gain in dBi is 2.15 dB higher
    C. Gain in dBd is 1.25 dBd lower
    D. Gain in dBd is 1.25 dBd higher

5. What is the primary effect of increasing boom length and adding directors to a Yagi antenna?
    A. Gain increases
    B. Beamwidth increases
    C. Front-to-back ratio decreases
    D. Resonant frequency is lower

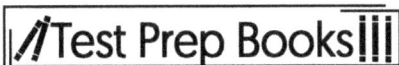

Subelement G9 – Antennas and Feed Lines

6. What does "front-to-back ratio" mean in reference to a Yagi antenna?
    A. The number of directors versus the number of reflectors
    B. The relative position of the driven element with respect to the reflectors and directors
    C. The power radiated in the major lobe compared to that in the opposite direction
    D. The ratio of forward gain to dipole gain

7. What is meant by the "main lobe" of a directive antenna?
    A. The magnitude of the maximum vertical angle of radiation
    B. The point of maximum current in a radiating antenna element
    C. The maximum voltage standing wave point on a radiating element
    D. The direction of maximum radiated field strength from the antenna

8. In free space, how does the gain of two three-element, horizontally polarized Yagi antennas spaced vertically 1/2 wavelength apart typically compare to the gain of a single three-element Yagi?
    A. Approximately 1.5 dB higher
    B. Approximately 3 dB higher
    C. Approximately 6 dB higher
    D. Approximately 9 dB higher

9. Which of the following can be adjusted to optimize forward gain, front-to-back ratio, or SWR bandwidth of a Yagi antenna?
    A. The physical length of the boom
    B. The number of elements on the boom
    C. The spacing of each element along the boom
    D. All these choices are correct

10. What is a beta or hairpin match?
    A. A shorted transmission line stub placed at the feed point of a Yagi antenna to provide impedance matching
    B. A 1/4 wavelength section of 75-ohm coax in series with the feed point of a Yagi to provide impedance matching
    C. A series capacitor selected to cancel the inductive reactance of a folded dipole antenna
    D. A section of 300-ohm twin-lead transmission line used to match a folded dipole antenna

11. Which of the following is a characteristic of using a gamma match with a Yagi antenna?
    A. It does not require the driven element to be insulated from the boom
    B. It does not require any inductors or capacitors
    C. It is useful for matching multiband antennas
    D. All these choices are correct

G9D

1. Which of the following antenna types will be most effective as a near vertical incidence skywave (NVIS) antenna for short-skip communications on 40 meters during the day?
    A. A horizontal dipole placed between 1/10 and 1/4 wavelength above the ground
    B. A vertical antenna placed between 1/4 and 1/2 wavelength above the ground
    C. horizontal dipole placed at approximately 1/2 wavelength above the ground
    D. A vertical dipole placed at approximately 1/2 wavelength above the ground

156

Subelement G9 – Antennas and Feed Lines

2. What is the feed point impedance of an end-fed half-wave antenna?
    A. Very low
    B. Approximately 50 ohms
    C. Approximately 300 ohms
    D. Very high

3. In which direction is the maximum radiation from a VHF/UHF "halo" antenna?
    A. Broadside to the plane of the halo
    B. Opposite the feed point
    C. Omnidirectional in the plane of the halo
    D. On the same side as the feed point

4. What is the primary function of antenna traps?
    A. To enable multiband operation
    B. To notch spurious frequencies
    C. To provide balanced feed point impedance
    D. To prevent out-of-band operation

5. What is an advantage of vertically stacking horizontally polarized Yagi antennas?
    A. It allows quick selection of vertical or horizontal polarization
    B. It allows simultaneous vertical and horizontal polarization
    C. It narrows the main lobe in azimuth
    D. It narrows the main lobe in elevation

6. Which of the following is an advantage of a log-periodic antenna?
    A. Wide bandwidth
    B. Higher gain per element than a Yagi antenna
    C. Harmonic suppression
    D. Polarization diversity

7. Which of the following describes a log-periodic antenna?
    A. Element length and spacing vary logarithmically along the boom
    B. Impedance varies periodically as a function of frequency
    C. Gain varies logarithmically as a function of frequency
    D. SWR varies periodically as a function of boom length

8. How does a "screwdriver" mobile antenna adjust its feed point impedance?
    A. By varying its body capacitance
    B. By varying the base loading inductance
    C. By extending and retracting the whip
    D. By deploying a capacitance hat

9. What is the primary use of a Beverage antenna?
    A. Directional receiving for MF and low HF bands
    B. Directional transmitting for low HF bands
    C. Portable direction finding at higher HF frequencies
    D. Portable direction finding at lower HF frequencies

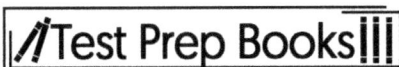

Subelement G9 – Antennas and Feed Lines

10. In which direction or directions does an electrically small loop (less than 1/10 wavelength in circumference) have nulls in its radiation pattern?
    A. In the plane of the loop
    B. Broadside to the loop
    C. Broadside and in the plane of the loop
    D. Electrically small loops are omnidirectional

11. Which of the following is a disadvantage of multiband antennas?
    A. They present low impedance on all design frequencies
    B. They must be used with an antenna tuner
    C. They must be fed with open wire line
    D. They have poor harmonic rejection

12. What is the common name of a dipole with a single central support?
    A. Inverted V
    B. Inverted L
    C. Sloper
    D. Lazy H

Subelement G9 – Answer Key

G9A

1. A	7. D
2. B	8. B
3. D	9. A
4. C	10. D
5. B	11. A
6. D	

G9B

1. B	7. B
2. B	8. A
3. D	9. A
4. A	10. D
5. C	11. C
6. C	12. A

G9C

1. A	7. D
2. B	8. B
3. A	9. D
4. B	10. A
5. A	11. A
6. C	

G9D

1. A	7. A
2. D	8. B
3. C	9. A
4. A	10. B
5. D	11. D
6. A	12. A

Subelement G0 – Electrical and RF Safety

G0A

RF Safety Principles, Rules, and Guidelines

RF (radio frequency) safety is an important consideration when operating any ham radio system, namely, to avoid RF radiation: a type of electromagnetic radiation that can be harmful to living organisms in large doses. Follow proper safety guidelines to ensure that you, other operators, and the public are protected from excessive RF exposure.

Among the most important principles of **RF safety** is to always operate within the guidelines established by regulatory agencies, such as the FCC. These guidelines set limits on the maximum allowable exposure to RF radiation based on the frequency of the signal, the duration of exposure, and other factors. Ham radio operators are required to follow these guidelines to ensure that they do not exceed safe levels of RF radiation.

Additionally, radio operators should always maintain distance from any antenna and transmission lines. The closer you are to the antenna or transmission lines, the higher the level of RF radiation you will be exposed to. It is important to keep a safe distance from these components, especially when they are in operation. Place warning signs or barriers around the antenna and transmission lines, and ensure that workstations are not built too closely to antenna and transmission lines.

Proper antenna installation is also crucial to RF safety. Antennae should be installed in a location that is inaccessible to the public and away from areas where people are likely to gather, such as playgrounds or swimming pools. Antennae should also be properly grounded to prevent the buildup of static electricity, which can increase the risk of electrical shock and RF exposure.

When working with high-power transmitters, take additional transmitter-specific precautions to ensure safety. High-power transmitters can generate high levels of RF radiation, which is why operators should wear appropriate personal protective equipment, such as RF shielding clothing, gloves, and goggles, when working with these systems. Furthermore, be aware of any potential hazards in the surrounding environment. For example, power lines and other sources of electromagnetic radiation can increase the risk of RF exposure, even if these sources do not directly relate to radios. Operators should be aware of these hazards and take steps to minimize their proximity to devices that threaten RF radiation.

In addition to these principles, there are several rules and guidelines regarding radio handling that ham radio operators should follow to ensure RF safety. For example, always use the lowest power level necessary to achieve a clear signal. This helps to conserve energy, minimize RF exposure, and reduce interference with other radio systems. Operators should also be careful not to accidentally key the microphone or activate the transmitter when making adjustments to the system. This can cause a sudden burst of high-power RF radiation, which can be dangerous.

When working with mobile or portable systems, properly secure the antenna and transmission lines to prevent them from coming into contact with people or other objects. It is also important with these systems, as it is in all radio systems, to follow any special instructions provided by the manufacturer regarding the safe use and operation of the equipment.

Subelement G0 – Electrical and RF Safety

Routine Station Evaluation

Ham radio stations must go through regular routine station evaluations for safety's sake. This involves a systematic check of all the equipment, antennae, and other components to ensure they are in good working order and meet the required standards. The evaluation can help to identify problems early on and prevent them from escalating into more significant issues that could affect the quality of communication.

A typical station evaluation involves checking the power output of the transmitter, the receiving sensitivity of the receiver, and the performance of any antennae. Checking the power output of the transmitter involves connecting a wattmeter to the output of the transmitter and making sure that the power output is within the specified range. A power output that is too low may indicate a problem with the transmitter, such as a faulty output stage or a blown fuse.

Receiving sensitivity of the receiver can be evaluated by monitoring weak signals and ensuring they are received clearly without any distortion or noise. This can be done by using an external signal generator to simulate a weak signal and checking the receiver's response.

Proper antenna performance can be evaluated by checking the SWR (standing wave ratio) of the antenna. As explained in G9A: Standing wave ratio (SWR) calculation, measurement, and effects, A high SWR indicates that the antenna is not properly matched to the transmitter and could lead to reduced signal strength and potential damage to the transmitter. Checking the SWR involves connecting an SWR meter between the transmitter and the antenna and monitoring the reading.

G0B

Station Safety: Electrical Shock, Safety Grounding, Fusing, Interlocks, and Wiring

Station safety protects primarily ham radio operators from electrical shock and equipment damage. The following are some of the important station safety measures that must be taken into consideration when setting up a ham radio station:

Electrical shock is among the most dangerous hazards of ham radio operations. It can result from a variety of causes, including improper grounding, touching exposed wires or components, and accidental contact with high-voltage sources. As such, all electrical components should be treated with care and respect, and any necessary precautions should be taken.

One of the most important measures to prevent electrical shock is to ensure that all equipment is properly grounded. Grounding helps to create a low-resistance path for current to flow to the earth in the event of a short circuit or electrical fault. To properly ground your station, install a ground rod or ground plate and connect all your equipment to it using copper wire or ground straps. The grounding system should be bonded to the AC electrical ground to create a common ground reference. A high-quality ground system can also help reduce noise and interference with your radio's signal. Furthermore, it is advisable to install fuses or circuit breakers in the power supply to protect the equipment from electrical faults.

Another crucial aspect of station safety is interlocks. An interlock is a safety device that prevents equipment from being energized or operated when specific conditions are not met. For example, a power amplifier might have an interlock that prevents the amplifier from being switched on if the antenna is not properly connected. This can help to prevent damage to both the amplifier and the antenna and reduces the risk of electrical shock among operators.

Proper wiring is also essential for station safety. All wiring should be tested and certified for the maximum current that it will carry, and it should be protected by fuses or circuit breakers. Wiring should be installed neatly and securely, and all connections should be tight and free from corrosion. When making connections and handling wires in general, ensure that the power is turned off, and always use insulated tools.

Ham radio operators should always be aware of the potential hazards associated with their equipment and take the necessary precautions to protect themselves and their radios. By following established safety guidelines and principles, ham radio operators can conduct their work and/or enjoy their hobby safely and without incident.

Antenna and Tower Safety

Antenna and tower safety is of paramount importance, as these components pose a significant risk not only of electrical shock, but also fall hazards and potentially catastrophic structural failures. Follow proper safety guidelines when installing, maintaining, or repairing them.

As is the case with general station safety, grounding is also critical for antennae and towers. Beyond the ways grounding was emphasized in "0B: Station safety: electrical shock, grounding, fusing, interlocks, wiring," grounding also helps prevent damage from lightning strikes, a danger to which antennae and towers are particularly susceptible. All conductive elements of the antenna system, including the tower, mast, coaxial cable, and any metal structures, should be connected to a grounding system. In turn, that system should be connected to a ground rod or other appropriate ground point, such as a metal water pipe or a grounding grid.

Furthermore, radio operators and electricians should ensure that all wiring and connections remain secure and in good condition. Connections that are loose, corroded, or damaged can cause interference, arcing, and electrical shocks. All connections should be inspected regularly and repaired or replaced as needed.

In addition to grounding and wiring, tower safety includes proper tower maintenance and inspection. Towers should be inspected regularly to ensure that all bolts and connections are secure and that there is no rust or other structural damage. Any damaged or corroded parts should be repaired or replaced before the tower is used.

Falls are a significant hazard in tower climbing. Anyone climbing a tower must use proper safety equipment, including a full-body harness, a fall-arrest system, and a safety helmet. Additionally, climbers should be trained in proper climbing techniques and have experience in tower climbing.

Subelement G0 – Questions

G0A

1. What is one way that RF energy can affect human body tissue?
   A. It heats body tissue
   B. It causes radiation poisoning
   C. It causes the blood count to reach a dangerously low level
   D. It cools body tissue

2. Which of the following is used to determine RF exposure from a transmitted signal?
   A. Its duty cycle
   B. Its frequency
   C. Its power density
   D. All these choices are correct

3. How can you determine that your station complies with FCC RF exposure regulations?
   A. By calculation based on FCC OET Bulletin 65
   B. By calculation based on computer modeling
   C. By measurement of field strength using calibrated equipment
   D. All these choices are correct

4. What does "time averaging" mean when evaluating RF radiation exposure?
   A. The average amount of power developed by the transmitter over a specific 24-hour period
   B. The average time it takes RF radiation to have any long-term effect on the body
   C. The total time of the exposure
   D. The total RF exposure averaged over a certain period

5. What must you do if an evaluation of your station shows that the RF energy radiated by your station exceeds permissible limits for possible human absorption?
   A. Take action to prevent human exposure to the excessive RF fields
   B. File an Environmental Impact Statement (EIS-97) with the FCC
   C. Secure written permission from your neighbors to operate above the controlled MPE limits
   D. All these choices are correct

6. What must you do if your station fails to meet the FCC RF exposure exemption criteria?
   A. Perform an RF Exposure Evaluation in accordance with FCC OET Bulletin 65
   B. Contact the FCC for permission to transmit
   C. Perform an RF exposure evaluation in accordance with World Meteorological Organization guidelines
   D. Use an FCC-approved band-pass filter

7. What is the effect of modulation duty cycle on RF exposure?
   A. A lower duty cycle permits greater power levels to be transmitted
   B. A higher duty cycle permits greater power levels to be transmitted
   C. Low duty cycle transmitters are exempt from RF exposure evaluation requirements
   D. High duty cycle transmitters are exempt from RF exposure requirements

8. Which of the following steps must an amateur operator take to ensure compliance with RF safety regulations?
   A. Post a copy of FCC Part 97.13 in the station
   B. Notify neighbors within a 100-foot radius of the antenna of the existence of the station and power levels
   C. Perform a routine RF exposure evaluation and prevent access to any identified high exposure areas
   D. All these choices are correct

9. What type of instrument can be used to accurately measure an RF field strength?
   A. A receiver with digital signal processing (DSP) noise reduction
   B. A calibrated field strength meter with a calibrated antenna
   C. An SWR meter with a peak-reading function
   D. An oscilloscope with a high-stability crystal marker generator

10. What should be done if evaluation shows that a neighbor might experience more than the allowable limit of RF exposure from the main lobe of a directional antenna?
    A. Change to a non-polarized antenna with higher gain
    B. Use an antenna with a higher front-to-back ratio
    C. Take precautions to ensure that the antenna cannot be pointed in their direction when they are present
    D. All these choices are correct

11. What precaution should be taken if you install an indoor transmitting antenna?
    A. Locate the antenna close to your operating position to minimize feed-line radiation
    B. Position the antenna along the edge of a wall to reduce parasitic radiation
    C. Make sure that MPE limits are not exceeded in occupied areas
    D. Make sure the antenna is properly shielded

12. What stations are subject to the FCC rules on RF exposure?
    A. All commercial stations; amateur radio stations are exempt
    B. Only stations with antennas lower than one wavelength above the ground
    C. Only stations transmitting more than 500 watts PEP
    D. All stations with a time-averaged transmission of more than one milliwatt

G0B

1. Which wire or wires in a four-conductor 240 VAC circuit should be attached to fuses or circuit breakers?
   A. Only the hot wires
   B. Only the neutral wire
   C. Only the ground wire
   D. All wires

Subelement G0 – Electrical and RF Safety

2. According to the National Electrical Code, what is the minimum wire size that may be used safely for wiring with a 20-ampere circuit breaker?
   A. AWG number 20
   B. AWG number 16
   C. AWG number 12
   D. AWG number 8

3. Which size of fuse or circuit breaker would be appropriate to use with a circuit that uses AWG number 14 wiring?
   A. 30 amperes
   B. 25 amperes
   C. 20 amperes
   D. 15 amperes

4. Where should the station's lightning protection ground system be located?
   A. As close to the station equipment as possible
   B. Outside the building
   C. Next to the closest power pole
   D. Parallel to the water supply line

5. Which of the following conditions will cause a ground fault circuit interrupter (GFCI) to disconnect AC power?
   A. Current flowing from one or more of the hot wires to the neutral wire
   B. Current flowing from one or more of the hot wires directly to ground
   C. Overvoltage on the hot wires
   D. All these choices are correct

6. Which of the following is covered by the National Electrical Code?
   A. Acceptable bandwidth limits
   B. Acceptable modulation limits
   C. Electrical safety of the station
   D. RF exposure limits of the human body

7. Which of these choices should be observed when climbing a tower using a safety harness?
   A. Always hold on to the tower with one hand
   B. Confirm that the harness is rated for the weight of the climber and that it is within its allowable service life
   C. Ensure that all heavy tools are securely fastened to the harness
   D. All these choices are correct

8. What should be done before climbing a tower that supports electrically powered devices?
   A. Notify the electric company that a person will be working on the tower
   B. Make sure all circuits that supply power to the tower are locked out and tagged
   C. Unground the base of the tower
   D. All these choices are correct

165

9. Which of the following is true of an emergency generator installation?
    A. The generator should be operated in a well-ventilated area
    B. The generator must be insulated from ground
    C. Fuel should be stored near the generator for rapid refueling in case of an emergency
    D. All these choices are correct

10. Which of the following is a danger from lead-tin solder?
    A. Lead can contaminate food if hands are not washed carefully after handling the solder
    B. High voltages can cause lead-tin solder to disintegrate suddenly
    C. Tin in the solder can "cold flow," causing shorts in the circuit
    D. RF energy can convert the lead into a poisonous gas

11. Which of the following is required for lightning protection ground rods?
    A. They must be bonded to all buried water and gas lines
    B. Bends in ground wires must be made as close as possible to a right angle
    C. Lightning grounds must be connected to all ungrounded wiring
    D. They must be bonded together with all other grounds

12. What is the purpose of a power supply interlock?
    A. To prevent unauthorized changes to the circuit that would void the manufacturer's warranty
    B. To shut down the unit if it becomes too hot
    C. To ensure that dangerous voltages are removed if the cabinet is opened
    D. To shut off the power supply if too much voltage is produced

13. Where should lightning arrestors be located?
    A. Where the feed lines enter the building
    B. On the antenna, opposite the feed point
    C. In series with each ground lead
    D. At the closest power pole ground electrode

Subelement G0 – Answer Key

G0A

1. A	7. A
2. D	8. C
3. D	9. B
4. D	10. C
5. A	11. C
6. A	12. D

G0B

1. A	8. B
2. C	9. A
3. D	10. A
4. B	11. D
5. B	12. C
6. C	13. A
7. B	

Index

11-Year Span, 59
28-Day Cycle, 59, 60, 69
60m (5 MHz) Band, 18
A Index, 62
Absorption, 11
AG, 21, 30
Airglow, 64
Alternating Current (AC), 11, 96, 108, 109
AM, 36, 45, 48, 64, 109, 128, 132, 133, 134, 136, 140, 143
Amateur Radio Digital Open Protocol (ARDOP), 45
Amateur Radio Emergency Data Networks (AREDNs), 22
Amateur Radio Relay League (ARRL, 20
Amateur Television (ATV), 12
Amazon Web Services (AWS), 45
Amplifiers, 121
Amplitude, 11, 36, 45, 93, 134, 139, 140
Amplitude Modulation (AM), 18, 132
Amplitude Shift Keying (ASK), 134
Analog IC, 111
Antenna, 13, 14, 17, 19, 25, 26, 27, 28, 35, 43, 46, 52, 54, 64, 66, 67, 75, 78, 80, 81, 83, 86, 87, 91, 92, 98, 99, 108, 111, 122, 135, 140, 142, 146, 147, 148, 149, 150, 151, 152, 153, 154, 155, 156, 158, 159, 160, 162, 164
Antenna Gain, 19
Ap, 62
Appleton Anomaly, 64
ASK, 134
Attenuation, 63, 67, 70, 129, 135, 146, 150
Audio Baseband Signal, 44
Audio Frequency Shift Keying (AFSK), 44
Audio Transformers, 99
Aurora Australis, 61
Aurora Borealis, 61
Auroral Oval, 61
Auroral Propagation, 61
Auroral Zones, 61
Auroras, 61, 64
Automated Repeat Query (ARQ), 45
Automatic Level Control (ALC), 36

Automatically Controlled Digital Station (ACDS, 23
Awaiting General, 21
Azimuthal Projection Map, 43, 52
Baluns, 99
Band Pass Filter, 19
Band Privileges, 12
Band-Pass Filter, 123, 130, 161
Bandwidth, 19, 142
Batteries, 110
Baud, 17
Baudot Code, 17, 143
Bd, 17
Beam Antennae, 148
Beverage Antennae, 149
Binary, 44, 45, 46, 111, 127, 139
Binary Code (1s and 0s), 44
Binary Frequency Shift Keying (BFSK), 44
Bits Per Second (Bps), 19
BNC Connectors, 112, 116
Bonding, 76, 77
Bridge Rectifiers, 108
Broadcasting, 15
Capacitance, 91
Capacitor, 80, 83, 98, 100, 104, 105, 107, 108, 114, 122, 154
Carrier Signal, 36, 44, 109, 122, 124, 132, 134, 136
Central Feed Line, 13
Central Frequencies, 19
Certificate of Successful Completion (CSCE), 21
Code of Federal Regulations (CFR), 14
Continuous Waveforms (CW), 15
Continuous Wavelength (CW) Mode, 39
Control Operator, 11, 15, 21, 22, 24, 25, 27, 28, 29, 31, 38, 44, 50, 54, 63
Corona, 60, 86
Coronal Hole, 59, 60, 69
Coronal Mass Ejections (CMEs), 60
CQ, 37, 39, 44, 48, 49, 51, 52, 54
CQ DX, 37, 48
CQD, 37
Critical Angle, 66, 72
Current Divider Circuits, 95

Cyclical, 59
D Layer (60km-90km), 66
Data Emissions, 17, 18
DE-9, 46
Decibel (DB), 93
Deviation, 136, 137
Diffraction, 11
Digital Emission Modes, 137, 138
Digital Gateways, 46
Digital ICs, 111
Digital Modulation, 121, 124, 134
Diode Rectifiers, 108
Dipole, 13, 19, 27, 28, 67, 147, 148, 149, 152, 153, 154, 156
Dipole Antenna, 147, 148, 152, 153, 154
Direct Current (DC), 11, 108, 109
Directional Antennae, 148
Discone Antennae, 149
Distance (DX), 58
Distortions, 66
Domestic Allocations, 18
Dummy Load, 17, 35, 102, 103
Dummy Loads, 35
Dynamo Effect, 59
E Layer (90km-150km), 66
Earth-Moon-Earth (EME), 45
Effective Radiated Power (ERP), 19
Electromagnetic Interference (EMI)., 113
Electromagnetic Radiation, 11
Electromagnetic Spectrum, 11, 58, 59
Electromagnetic Waves, 11
Envelope, 36, 82, 109, 133
F Layer, 66, 67
F1 (150km-220km), 66
F2 (220km-800km), 66
Federal Aviation Administration (FAA), 13
Federal Communications Commission (FCC), 12
Federal Emergency Management Agency (FEMA), 38
Feed Point Matching, 147
Ferrite Cores, 113
Filters, 108, 111, 113, 122, 123, 124, 137
FM, 16, 45, 54, 109, 128, 132, 133, 134, 136, 137, 139, 141
FM Repeater, 16, 54
Fox Hunting, 43

Frequency, 11, 12, 17, 44, 45, 47, 63, 70, 71, 107, 128, 134, 135, 136, 139, 140, 141, 144
Frequency Band, 12, 13, 15, 16, 17, 36, 48, 59, 63, 123, 133, 136, 149
Frequency Changing, 135, 136
Frequency Hopping, 22
Frequency Modulation (FM), 18, 109, 123, 132
Frequency Privileges, 12
Frequency Shift Keying (FSK), 44
FSK, 44, 45, 55, 121, 134, 137, 139, 144
FT8, 44, 45, 54, 55, 137, 140, 143, 144
Full Break-In Operation (QSK), 41
Geomagnetic Field, 59, 61, 68, 69
Geomagnetic Indices, 61, 62
Geomagnetic Storms, 59, 60
Global Scale Observations of the Limb and Disk (GOLD), 64
Goertzel Algorithm, 44
Goldwater-Wirth Bill, 20
Grey Line or Terminator, 66
Grounding, 76, 77, 159, 160
Groundwave Propagation, 64, 66
Harmful Interference, 13, 22, 24, 31, 49
Helical Antennae, 149
Heliosphere, 60, 61
Hertz, 11, 19
Hertz (Hz), 19
Hidden Transmitter Hunts, 43
High-Pass Filter, 108, 123
Impedance, 13, 83, 85, 91, 92, 98, 100, 107, 108, 147, 155
Impedance Transformation, 92, 98
Incident Angle, 66, 67
Inductance, 48, 76, 91, 98, 100, 103, 104, 105, 113, 114, 116, 127, 155
Inductance-Capacitance (L-C) Meter, 76
Inductor, 83, 98, 100, 104, 105, 108, 113, 115, 116, 122, 126
Inductors, 98, 108, 110, 122
Industrial, Scientific, and Medical (ISM), 22
Integrated Circuits (ICs), 111
Interference, 13, 22, 23, 24, 38, 41, 42, 45, 47, 49, 50, 51, 59, 75, 76, 80, 83, 84, 87, 108, 112, 119, 121, 122, 123, 132, 133, 134, 135, 137, 138, 141, 143, 147, 148, 149, 158, 159, 160
Intermodulation, 137, 142

International Amateur Radio Union (IARU), 15
International Aviation or NATO Alphabet, 35
International Beacon Project (IBP), 15, 22
International Space Station (ISS), 64
International Telecommunication Union (ITU), 12
International Telecommunications Union, 23
Ionosphere, 13, 58, 59, 60, 61, 63, 64, 65, 66, 67, 70, 135
Ionospheric Connection Explorer (ICON), 64
Ionospheric Refraction, 65
Isotropic Antenna, 19, 28
JT65, 44, 45, 54, 136, 137, 138
K Index, 62
Kp, 62
Light-Emitting Diode (LED), 112
Line B, 23
Line of Sight Propagation, 64
Linear Power Supplies, 119
Link Budget, 135, 140
Link Margin, 135, 140
Liquid Crystal Display (LCD), 112
Load, 17, 35, 36, 92, 95, 101, 103, 107, 108, 125, 151
Log-Periodic Antenna, 148, 155
Long Path, 65, 69, 72
Loop Antennae, 149
Lower Side Band (LSB), 78
Lower Sideband (LSB), 19, 36
Lowest Usable Frequency (LUF), 63
Low-Pass Filter, 84, 123, 129
Magnetic Reconnection, 61
Magnetometer, 62
Magnetosphere, 59, 60, 61, 62, 72
Mark Frequencies, 44
Maximum Power Theorem, 91, 92
Maximum Usable Frequency (MUF), 36, 63
Memory Channel, 16
Microwave ICs (MMICs), 111
Modem, 45, 46, 54
Modulating, 45
Modulation, 45, 46, 110, 122, 129, 133, 140
Modulation Envelope, 133, 134, 140
Monopole Antenna, 147, 148, 153
Moonbounce Paths, 45
Multi-Hop Propagation, 66
Multimeter, 76, 82

Multipath Distortion, 67
Mutual Capacitance, 91
N Connectors, 112
Nano Vector Network Analyzer (VNA), 76
National Telecommunications and Information Agency (NTIA), 18
Near Vertical Incidence Skywave (NVIS), 67
Northern California DX Foundation (NCDXF), 15
NVIS Antennas, 67
NVIS Dipoles, 67
Official Observers (OO), 43
Ohm's Law, 95, 96
Ohms, 13, 17, 150
Operational Modes, 12
Organic Light-Emitting Diode (OLED), 112
Oscillators, 44, 108, 109, 110, 121, 122, 123
Oscilloscope, 17, 81, 82, 162
Overmodulation, 46, 134, 144
Packet Teleprinting on Radio (PACTOR), 45
Part 97, 14, 15, 17, 22, 26, 27, 32, 43, 162
Partial Element Credit, 21
Peak Envelope Power, 17, 97
Peak Envelope Power (PEP), 17
Peak Envelope Voltage, 97
Phase Shift Key, 31 Baud (PSK31), 46
Phase Shift Keying, 137
Phase Shift Keying (PSK), 134
Phone Operation, 12, 24
Phonetic Alphabet, 35, 37, 44
Pileup, 37
Planetary A Index, 62
Planetary K Index, 62
Plasma, 58, 59, 60, 64, 66
Polar Binary Baseband Signal, 44
Polar Cap Absorption (PCA), 59
Power Law, 95, 96, 97
Power Line Carriers (PLCs), 17
Power Meters, 76
Power Supply, 39, 75, 78, 79, 81, 108, 116, 119, 125, 126, 128, 159, 164
Primary Allocations, 13
Procedure Sign, 39
Propagation, 11, 13, 15, 16, 22, 26, 32, 36, 38, 49, 54, 58, 59, 60, 61, 62, 63, 64, 65, 66, 67, 68, 69, 70, 71, 72, 73, 77, 83, 142, 144
Prosign, 39, 50, 51
PSK, 81, 121, 124, 134, 137

Push to Talk (PTT), 37
Q Signals, 39, 40, 75
Q-Code, 35, 37
Q-Signals, 39
QSO, 35, 36, 37, 42
Quadrature, 46, 124
Quarter-Wave Vertical Antenna, 148
Radiation Storm, 60, 61
Radio Amateur Civil Emergency Service (RACES), 38
Radio Antennas, 13
Radio Blackouts, 60, 61
Radio Direction Finding (RDF), 67
Radio Frequency (RF), 11, 109, 111, 122
Radio Mail Server (RMS) Express, 45
Radio Propagation Beacon, 15
Radio Shorthand, 39
Radio Spectrum, 11, 18, 22
Radio Teletype, 137
Radio Waves, 11
Radioteletype (RTTY), 17, 44
Reactance, 91, 100, 141
Readability, Strength, and Tone, 39
Rectifiers, 108, 109, 110
Reflection, 11
Refraction, 11, 65
Region 1, 23, 31
Region 2, 23, 31
Region 3, 23, 31
Repeaters, 12, 16
Resistor, 88, 94, 95, 98, 102, 103, 107, 114, 125
Resonance, 92, 101
RF Chokes, 113
RF Safety, 158, 162
Root Mean Square (Rms), 17
Root-Mean-Square, 96
RST, 39, 51
RST Report, 39, 51
RTTY, 17, 18, 19, 23, 28, 32, 44, 45, 46, 53, 54, 55, 81, 136, 137, 143, 144
RTTY Demodulator, 18
S Meter, 51, 78, 85, 86
Scatter Signals, 67
Scattering, 11
Schematic Symbols, 119
Secondary Services, 13
Self-Capacitance, 91

Short Path, 52, 65, 72
Shortwave Bands, 12, 19, 58
Sidebands, 36, 78, 128, 132, 133, 136
Signal Jamming, 67
Single Sideband (SSB), 18
Single Sideband Modulation (SSB), 132
Skip, 66
Skip Zone, 66, 67, 72
Skywave Propagation, 63, 65, 66, 67
Skywave Refraction, 58
Skywaves, 58, 66
Slow Scan Television (SSTV), 12
SMA Connectors, 112
Smoothed Sunspot Number (SSN), 61
Solar Cycle, 58, 59, 60, 61, 69
Solar Filaments, 60
Solar Flares, 58, 59
Solar Flux Index (SFI), 61
Solar Flux Units (SFUs), 61
Solar Indices, 61
Solar Maximum, 59
Solar Minimum, 59
Solar Radiation, 58, 66, 70
Solar Wind Particles, 60
Solar Winds, 60
Solid-State Diodes, 109
Space Frequencies, 44, 55
Speech Processors, 77
Spread Spectrum Transmissions, 22
Spurious Emission, 17
SSB Modulation, 133, 134
Standing Wave Ratio (SWR), 146, 159
Station Log, 31, 44, 53
Sudden Disappearing Filament (SDF), 60
Sudden Ionospheric Disturbance (SID), 59
Sunspot Number (SN), 61
Sunspots, 58
Suppressed Carrier Frequencies, 19
Switching Power Supplies, 119
Symbol Rate, 17, 18, 28, 142
Table of Frequency Allocations, 13
the Volunteer Monitor Program, 43
Third-Party Traffic, 22
Title 47, 14
Transceiver, 16, 37, 44, 46, 48, 75, 81, 85, 87, 117, 122, 123, 128
Transceiver Channel, 16

Transformer, 92, 98, 101, 103, 104, 109, 119, 125, 126, 128
Transistors, 109
Transmission Lines, 11, 158
Transmission Switches, 37
Transmitters, 11, 136
True Bearings, 43, 52
UHF Connectors, 112
Upper Side Band (USB), 78
    Upper Sideband (USB), 18, 19, 36
USB, 18, 19, 27, 36, 44, 46, 53, 54, 86, 133
USB-to-Serial Adaptor, 46
Utilities Technology Council (UTC), 17
Vacuum Tube Rectifiers, 108
Vacuum Tubes, 109, 110
VARA HF, 45, 46
Varicode Character Schematic, 46
Vertical Arrays, 149
Voice Operated Exchange (VOX), 37
Voice Operated Relay, 37
Voice Operated Switch, 37
Voltage Divider Circuits, 94
Voltage Transformers, 99
Voluntary Band Plan, 38, 49
Volunteer Examiner Coordinator (VEC), 20
Volunteer Examiner Manual, 21
Volunteer Examiners (VEs), 20
Volunteer Monitors, 43
Waterfall Display, 46, 144
Wavelength, 11, 12
Weak Signal Propagation Reporter, 15
Weather Facsimile (WEFAX), 12
Winlink, 45, 53, 55, 144
WINMOR, 45
Wolf Number, 61
WSJT, 44
WSPR, 15, 142, 144
Yagi-Uda Antenna, 148
Zero Beat, 39, 51

Dear Ham Radio Test Taker,

Thank you again for purchasing this study guide for your Ham Radio exam. We hope that we exceeded your expectations.

Our goal in creating this study guide was to cover all of the topics that you will see on the test. We also strove to make our practice questions as similar as possible to what you will encounter on test day. With that being said, if you found something that you feel was not up to your standards, please send us an email and let us know.

Thanks Again and Happy Testing!
Product Development Team
support@testprepbooks.com

Online Resources

Included with your purchase are multiple online resources. This includes the practice tests in an interactive format and a convenient study timer to help you manage your time.

Scan the QR code or go to this link to access this content:

testprepbooks.com/online387/ham-radio

The first time you access the page, you will need to register as a "new user" and verify your email address.

If you have any issues, please email support@testprepbooks.com.

Thank you for letting us be a part of your studying journey!